How to Write Good Programs

Learning to program isn't just learning the details of a programming language: to become a good programmer you have to become expert at debugging, testing, writing clear code and generally unsticking yourself when you get stuck, while to do well in a programming course you have to learn to score highly in coursework and exams.

Featuring tips, stories and explanations of key terms, this book teaches these skills explicitly. Examples in Python, Java and Haskell are included, helping you to gain transferable programming skills whichever language you are learning. Intended for students in Higher or Further Education studying early programming courses, it will help you succeed in, and get the most out of, your course and support you in developing the software engineering habits that lead to good programs.

Perdita Stevens is a professor at the University of Edinburgh and has taught programming and software engineering in many languages to students ranging from first-year undergraduates to established professional software developers. She previously co-authored *Using UML: Software Engineering with Objects and Components* (1998) and received a 10-year Most Influential Paper award and a Best Paper award at the MODELS conference in 2017 for her ~~~~ ~~~~ ~~~~ c-tional transformations.

T0275203

How to Write Good Programs

A Guide for Students

PERDITA STEVENS

CAMBRIDGE
UNIVERSITY PRESS

CAMBRIDGE
UNIVERSITY PRESS

University Printing House, Cambridge CB2 8BS, United Kingdom

One Liberty Plaza, 20th Floor, New York, NY 10006, USA

477 Williamstown Road, Port Melbourne, VIC 3207, Australia

314–321, 3rd Floor, Plot 3, Splendor Forum, Jasola District Centre,
New Delhi – 110025, India

79 Anson Road, #06–04/06, Singapore 079906

Cambridge University Press is part of the University of Cambridge.

It furthers the University's mission by disseminating knowledge in the pursuit of
education, learning, and research at the highest international levels of excellence.

www.cambridge.org
Information on this title: www.cambridge.org/9781108789875
DOI: 10.1017/9781108804783

First published 2020

Printed in the United Kingdom by TJ International Ltd. Padstow Cornwall

A catalogue record for this publication is available from the British Library.

Library of Congress Cataloging-in-Publication Data
Names: Stevens, Perdita, author.
Title: How to write good programs : a guide for students / Perdita Stevens.
Description: New York : Cambridge University Press, 2020. |
Includes bibliographical references and index.
Identifiers: LCCN 2020003584 (print) | LCCN 2020003585 (ebook) |
ISBN 9781108804783 (epub) | ISBN 9781108789875 (hardback)
Subjects: LCSH: Computer programming–Textbooks.
Classification: LCC QA76.73.P98 (ebook) |
LCC QA76.73.P98 S74 2020 (print) | DDC 005.13–dc23

ISBN 978-1-108-78987-5 Paperback

Contents

1

Introduction

This book assumes that you are committed to learning to program, and want to do well. Most likely, you are taking a programming course in college or university. Perhaps you don't have much experience programming yet, or perhaps you have programmed a fair bit, but now you are interested in how to improve the quality of the programs you write. This book aims to help you learn how to write *good* programs, in any language. It's the book I wish I'd had available to me, nearly forty years ago when I started programming; and the book I wish I could have recommended to my students, especially my first-year undergraduate students, over many years since.

Let us tackle one thing head on. People sometimes talk as though students could be divided into programming sheep and non-programming goats: as though programming ability were innate. My experience over more than twenty-five years of teaching, and most current research, suggests that this is *simply not true*. I have lost count of the number of times I have seen students really struggle to begin with, perhaps even failing their first programming course, but go on to become excellent programmers. It also sometimes happens that people come in feeling very confident, perhaps having more programming experience than most of those around them, and later realise that they had hardly begun to tackle the most interesting challenges in software development.

Some people love programming from the very beginning. These people may have started coding at a young age, and often choose to sit up late into the night doing so. That's great, and if you're one of them, I hope you will benefit from this book. But, full disclosure: I was not one of those people. Indeed, when, as a child, I was first introduced to programming, I didn't really see the point. I didn't start to spend a lot of time on programming until, in my twenties, I encountered a problem I couldn't solve without writing a program. I learned to program because I had a problem I needed to solve, which I couldn't solve any other way.

Tip

To write good programs, you don't *have to* love programming. Moreover, even people who love programming do not automatically write good programs: everyone has to learn how.

The great thing is that there's a virtuous cycle. The better your programs get, the more fun it is to write them.

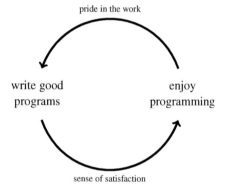

Perhaps you think it will take longer to write your programs so that they are good, and wonder whether this is something you want to invest in. Surprisingly, as you will discover through using this book, writing good programs *saves* you time and effort, compared with writing any old programs. If you like, you can spend that time and effort on writing more programs. If not, you can spend it on something else.

This book will not teach you any particular programming language – for that you will need a different book, a course, or an online tutorial, and there are plenty to choose from. This book will help you in the process of learning any programming language, and especially, it will help you to learn to write it *well*, and with deep understanding that you can also transfer to your next language. It covers things that programming courses tend to assume students will pick up by osmosis, but that are often, in practice, stumbling blocks. Unlike books aimed at professionals, which assume you can always express what you want to express in the language, this book will help you develop ways of getting unstuck, unconfused and debugged.

You'll learn to write code that you can understand and modify not only when you are at your cleverest, but also when you're not. This will lower your stress levels. It'll let you be lazy, in the best possible way.

There's a certain satisfaction in doing a thing well, though: that's how the virtuous circle works.

Robert Martin, in his wonderful book for professional software developers, *Clean Code*, talks about programmers needing to have "code sense". Code sense is what lets a seasoned professional tell good code from bad, and, much harder, systematically develop good code. If you are starting out with programming, this is what you need to develop. You won't develop it in a day, a week, or a year, but, by paying attention in the way this book aims to encourage, you will gradually increase your code sense.

1.1 Who Is This Book For?

If you are learning to program, this book is for you.

If you are helping other people to learn to program, this book is for you.

If you are a professional programmer, this book is not intended for you – but you are welcome to read it anyway. Perhaps you would like to recommend it to someone. I'd welcome your comments.

1.2 About the Boxes

We use various kinds of boxes. There are tips, like this one:

> **Tip**
>
> A note on spelling. If you spell in British English, you may expect the spelling "programme" rather than "program". However, by long convention, when we write about computer programs, we use the American spelling. Very, very occasionally this is useful disambiguation; computer science events may involve both programs and a programme. Normally, it's just one of those things you have to know.

Explanations of terms, like this:

> **Terminology: Coding, programming, software engineering**
>
> *Coding*, *programming* and *software engineering* overlap, and all involve giving a computer instructions. They are in increasing order of sophistication. A software engineer can program, and a programmer can code, but not necessarily the other way round. A coder might only translate precise English instructions into a programming language. A programmer takes responsibility for deciding what to write and when it is good. A software engineer typically works as part of a team, and solves real-world problems with high-quality software.

After absorbing the content of this book, you will be well equipped to progress to software engineering: more on that in Chapter 15.

There are stories, like this:

Story

Some people are hooked by programming from the very first time they meet the idea. I wasn't one of those. I thought it was quite cute that you could do things like writing programs to output a list of prime numbers, but I was never interested in writing video games, which, when I was young, looked like the only other thing you could do with a computer. The first program I really cared about was one I wrote when I was doing my PhD in mathematics. I had a conjecture that I thought was true for all integers n (it was to do with a certain collection of esoteric mathematical structures, the Weyl modules for $GL(2, \mathbb{Q})$). The calculations to check it got too tedious to do by hand after about $n = 5$, though. So I wrote a program to check my conjecture, and was quite easily able to find out that my conjecture was true, at least, for all n up to 10,000. Of course that wasn't a proof, but it gave me confidence to look for a proof, and eventually, I found one.

And, of course, there are examples of programs. Here's one example in Python:

Python example

```
print("Hello, World!")
```

Note that programs are not always complete. For example, Java code has to be inside a method inside a class, but I usually omit the lines that show that, writing

Java example

```
System.out.println("Hello, World!");
```

rather than something like

Java example

```
public class HelloWorld {
    public static void main(String[] args) {
        System.out.println("Hello, World!");
    }
}
```

Do not worry if any of the program examples do not immediately make sense to you, but do have a look at them. This book is supposed to support whatever language you are learning – only occasionally are there points that are really specific to one language. You will probably find that you can get the gist of an example in a language you do not know, if you read it in conjunction with the surrounding text. Learning to think beyond the confines of whatever language you are studying at present, and to transfer your skills between languages, is an important part of becoming a good software developer. If you are at the beginning of a programming career, the language you will use most may not even have been invented yet. I have chosen to include examples in Java, Python and Haskell: these are all common languages for early programming courses, and they contrast interestingly with one another, so that between them they allow us to cover a lot of ground.

In order to guide you to further reading, and to information that will help you fit what you are learning into the context of the programming language you are learning, there are often suggestions for things to put into your favourite search engine, like this:

 some language issue *your_language*

1.3 Structure of This Book

The nature of learning to program is that you will improve many skills in parallel; yet the nature of a book is that chapters need topics. I have tried to include many cross-references between the chapters, while leaving you plenty of freedom to dip into the book as and when you wish.

Chapters 1 (you're reading that now) to 3 get us going. Chapter 4 will help you to place the language you are learning in the landscape of all programming languages. Chapters 5 to 11 are the heart of the book; you're likely to flip between these chapters frequently. Chapters 12 and 13 are specifically about how to do well in a programming course; you might skip these entirely if, for example, you are teaching yourself to program. Chapters 14 and 15 are the farewell chapters, setting the scene for what I hope will be your lifetime of writing good programs.

1.4 Acknowledgements

I am very grateful to all of my students, colleagues and friends who have commented on drafts of this book, including the following: Alejandra Amaro Patiño; Paul Anderson; Julian Bradfield; Robin Bradfield; Carina Fiedler; Vashti Galpin; Lilia Georgieva; Jeremy Gibbons; Kris Hildrum; Lu-Shan Lee; James McKinna; Greg Michaelson; Hugh Pumphrey; Don Sannella; Jennifer Tenzer; Tom Ward.

Thanks are also due to all at Cambridge University Press, especially my editor David Tranah, and to the anonymous readers for helpful suggestions.

Of course, all remaining errors are mine. Feedback would be most welcome.

Perdita Stevens
phowto@stevens-bradfield.com

2

What Are Good Programs?

A book that discusses how to write good programs had better say what good programs are. That depends quite a lot on the context, and we'll have more to say about that in Chapter 10: but for now, let us begin at the beginning with the least controversial criterion.

Criterion 1

Good programs do what they are supposed to do.

That is, they are *correct*. If your program does the wrong thing, it isn't good – yet. This is the main topic of much of this book, especially Chapters 7 and 9.

Whenever you need to change your program, though – whether that's because it doesn't do what it should do yet, or because what it should do has changed since you first wrote it – you will care about some further criteria.

Criterion 2

Good programs are clearly written.

That is, they are as easy to read and understand as they can be. This is the topic of Chapter 8 – and throughout the book, we will be discussing how writing your program clearly helps you to make it correct.

You will often hear people talk as though they think

Criterion 3

¿Good programs are concise?

This one is sort of true – clearly written programs do tend to be concise, not least because they tend to avoid code duplication. That is, they deliver a lot of functionality in a small number of lines of code. However, this is not a good thing to aim for *in its own right* – rather, it should be a consequence of writing clear, correct code. It often happens that people over-value making their code concise, and end up making it less clear than it could have been.

If you are in the main target group for this book, and are taking a programming course, you probably cannot avoid this definition:

Criterion 4

Good programs get high marks.

This is the specific topic of Chapters 12 and 13. Of course, it is to be hoped that high marks are a side-effect of your programs being good in other respects …

Many other criteria matter sometimes: good programs often need to be fast, portable, flexible, testable, memory-efficient, parallelisable, and so on. We will look at some of these briefly in Chapter 10, but for the most part, specifically addressing these criteria is beyond the scope of this book: rather, we will emphasise that keeping your program correct and clear is the key to achieving all of them. Our final chapters, Chapters 14 and 15, may help to lead you into those more advanced areas.

2.1 Ethics

As a counterweight to the "get high marks" criterion let us finish this chapter on a serious note. Computers are everywhere these days, and this means that qualities of programs influence everything from whether our games are fun, via whether our privacy is preserved, to whether we live or die. Writing good programs really matters. Because of this, professional software developers – and others – are, increasingly, expected to abide by written codes of practice. These say more than just "write good programs", although absorbing the content of this book is a big step in the right direction. Ethical programming includes being honest about the extent to which you can be confident that your program is good, and adhering to quality control processes that ensure that if a mistake has been made – everybody makes mistakes – it is found and rectified before it causes harm. It also includes being a decent human being: for example, the software industry has a sexism problem, and you should strive to be part of the solution.

For more information, including codes of professional practice, search

 programming ethics

3

How to Get Started

In this chapter we assume you are about to do the first exercise in a programming course, or, perhaps, are starting to teach yourself a new language. In any case, you are about to create a program. You may have been given step-by-step instructions, but read this chapter all the same: it will set those instructions in context, and point out things that are easy to miss.

3.1 What Is a Program Anyway?

Terminology: Program

A *program* is a set of instructions that you would like a computer to follow.

Arguably, it's better to think of the program as being *an* instruction which may have complex structure. We're definitely not using the word "set" here in the same way you may have encountered it in mathematics: rather, we're using it in an everyday English sense. Other examples of sets of instructions are cooking recipes, or the leaflets you get with Lego kits or self-assembly furniture. However, while those are typically simple *lists* of instructions, telling you to do one thing, then another, a program can have more interesting structure. The way the parts of a program combine to make a whole is one of the things that varies between languages, and that you have to learn in the setting of a particular language.

A computer is a machine: it will follow your instructions blindly, with total, stupid obedience. Before it can do so, though, your instructions will be translated (by other programs, including a *compiler* or an *interpreter*), from the form in which you write them (the program), into a form which is capable of affecting the computer hardware (ultimately, binary code, zeroes and ones). That translation process – about which we will have more to say in Chapter 4 – naturally makes your life much more convenient; it is much easier to write in a modern programming language than in binary code. However, the very convenience of it may tempt you to forget how stupid the computer really is. If one of the translation steps involves rejecting most of your mistakes, it's easy to end up thinking that if the program gets to the point of being run, that means that the computer "understood" it, will "see what you mean", will do something sensible. That's an illusion – one that can be helpful, but that you need to see as fiction.

A computer (even with all its software running) is not an intelligence: not a friend, not a foe. It is just a machine. Learning to program involves understanding how to make that machine do what you want it to do.

3.2 What Do You Need?

So, a program is a set of instructions, which will eventually be translated into a form that can be run on computer hardware. You will need

1. a way to express the instructions;
2. a way to get them run on the computer hardware.

Let's consider the second point first. Unless this has already been done for you, or you are using a purely online system, you will probably need to *install* some software for your language by downloading something from the web. Precisely what you have to do depends on the language you are learning and on the computer you are using. Searching

install *your_language*

will usually help you find specific instructions. Chapter 4 will say more about how and why the process of getting to run your program varies between languages: you may also like to search

 getting started *your_language*

> **Tip**
>
> Some languages (at the time of writing, Python is a notable example) have several significantly different versions available. A program that is correct in one version of the language might be incorrect in another. Check you are installing the same version that your course uses.

Next, you need a way to express your instructions. It's just possible you're using a graphical programming language such as Scratch, in which case you'll do this by manipulating elements in an application specific to that language. Usually, though, you will type your instructions: we'll say you're going to *write* a program. Where do you type, though? There are three main possibilities:

1. at an interactive prompt;
2. into a file created with a text editor;
3. into a file held in an integrated development environment (IDE).

> **Terminology: Integrated development environment**
>
> An *integrated development environment* or IDE is an application that supports the whole process of developing a program.

IDEs are covered in Chapter 5: in this chapter we will discuss the more elementary options.

3.2.1 Using an Interactive Prompt

In some languages – including Python and Haskell, but not Java – you may start off exploring your language at some kind of interactive prompt, sometimes called a read-eval-print loop or REPL. After installing your language, you start its interactive tool, perhaps by typing a command at an operating system command line. The result is that you get a language-level interactive prompt. Do not confuse the two kinds of prompt: they understand different inputs. The operating system command line understands, for example, the instruction to start an application. The language-level interactive prompt expects something that makes sense in the programming language context. Here is an example of interacting with Python, and with Haskell, at their interactive prompts ("[...]" represents some output that isn't interesting, and will depend on your machine):

Python example

```
Python 3.7.3 [...]
>>> 3+4
7
>>>
```

Haskell example

```
GHCi, version 8.4.3: [...]
Prelude> 3+4
7
Prelude>
```

(So far, Python and Haskell agree – good!)

Jupyter notebooks[1] give a somewhat similar experience to using an interactive prompt. A notebook can mix formatted text and code, which makes it a convenient way for instructors to guide students through the early stages of programming. It's also a popular way to share data and ways of processing it. However, Jupyter notebooks are not very convenient for serious code development, and I would not advise adopting them unless you are on a course which supports it.

3.2.2 Using a Text Editor

An interactive prompt, on its own, is only good enough for very basic exploration, such as where you want to try out the effect of just one line of program code. The next step up is to save your program in a file, and edit it using a text editor. (Later, you may load your file at the interactive prompt to test and improve your code.) If you already have a favourite text editor, open it, and skip on to the next section . . .

. . . but these days, many people who are new to programming have experience with so-called WYSIWYG word processors such as Microsoft Word, but not with text editors. The line between word processors and text editors can get blurred, but fundamentally, a text editor operates on a file as a list of characters. When you save a file in a text editor, you know exactly what you're saving, because it's the same list of characters you see in the text editor. A word processor, even operating on a document that is basically just text, saves a lot more information about how you want the text to *look*: what fonts you have chosen, for example. The effect is that you usually have to open a file that has been written by a word processor in that same word processor in future. A text editor saves

---

1 https://jupyter.org/

a plain text file, which can be read and edited by any other text editor. Programming tools expect plain text files as their program inputs, although such files are usually given a specific suffix such as .java, .hs, or .py, instead of .txt, to indicate that what's in the file is, in fact, a program in a specific language.

Organising your files

Files are grouped into a hierarchical – tree-shaped – system of *directories* or *folders* (you may meet either or both terms, depending on your operating system: they mean the same thing). You will have, at least, a home directory to begin with; you can create your own subdirectories to organise your files. For example, if you are doing a course called Programming 1, you might find it convenient to create a subdirectory of your home directory called Programming1 and keep all the programs you write for this course in there. When you start working on Exercise 3 for the course, you might like to create a new subdirectory of Programming1, called Exercise3, for those specific program files. If you run a tool, such as an editor, by invoking it from a command line, you will need to make sure that you are in the right *current directory* for what you want to do, so that the tool finds the files you want to work on, without you having to give it complex directions to them. If this is not already familiar to you, use search terms such as

🔍 command line *your_operating_system*

🔍 change directory *your_operating_system*

Every modern computer comes with at least one text editor already available. On Windows, you'll find Notepad; on a Mac,

TextEdit; on Linux, vi or (better, if available[2]) Emacs. You may as well start with whatever you have. Later, you can either switch to any text editor you prefer – besides Emacs, Atom and Sublime are popular ones available on many platforms, and on Windows many developers like Notepad++ – or to an integrated development environment (IDE) (see Chapter 5). You can open and save a file using menu options, and it will probably be pretty obvious how to do basic editing. As soon as you have trouble, searching

  your_editor_name tutorial

is a good move.

3.3 Understanding What You Have to Do

In an early programming exercise, you may be given a template file that contains some of the program already. In this case, instead of having to write the whole program, you simply have to fill in some missing bits. For example, early in a Haskell course, you might be given the following file:

Haskell example

```
say :: Integer -> String
say = undefined

main :: IO()
main = mapM_ putStrLn $ map say [1..100]
```

and the instruction

---

2 That's what passes for a joke among computer scientists. With it I declare my allegiance in the *editor wars* – you could do a search for that, or trust me . . .

Fizz Buzz exercise

Your Haskell program should print out the numbers 1 to 100, each on a new line, except that:

* each number that is divisible by 3 must be replaced by "Fizz";
* each number that is divisible by 5 must be replaced by "Buzz";
* each number that is divisible by both 3 and 5 must be replaced by "FizzBuzz".

You are given the function `main` which will apply the function `say` to each number in turn, and print the results. Your task is to write the function `say`. For example

* `say 1` returns "1"
* `say 10` returns "Buzz"
* `say 30` returns "FizzBuzz"

Template files are used because you can't teach, or learn, everything at once; in this example, the definition of `main` involves things you would not normally learn in the first week of a Haskell course. Still:

Tip

Whenever you are given code to use, take advantage of the chance to learn from it. How much can you understand, and can you identify specific things you don't understand yet?

If you are not given a template file, your question probably says – perhaps after some introductory text – something like:

Write a class Name to . . .

Write a function to . . .

Write a program to . . .

For example, a different version of the Fizz Buzz exercise might
begin:

Fizz Buzz exercise

Write a Python function called `fizz_buzz` that takes an integer n and prints out the numbers from 1 to n, each on a new
line, except that ... *[instructions as before]*

Before you put fingers to keyboard, read through any such
instructions carefully, making sure that you understand what is
required. Remember that, because the computer is just a machine,
details such as names can be important. If you are going to write a
function, you may be told what it should return in one case. Check
your understanding by working out what it should return in one or
two other cases. Make a note, electronically or on paper – you can
use these cases as tests later.

3.4 Writing Your Program

Tip

The biggest mistake that beginning programmers make is writing too much code before checking it works.

In the early days of computing, programmers used to have to
produce punched cards and send them away to be run overnight,
but you are probably more fortunate! If you're in *any* doubt about
your ability to write your whole program correctly first time, you
will save time overall if you split the work up into tiny chunks, and
check each chunk is working as you expect, before you go on. Often
a good tip is to work from the outside in, writing a skeleton of your

code first, then filling in the details. If you have to write a class, or a function, what is the syntax for that?

Terminology: Syntax and semantics

Roughly speaking[a], the *syntax* of a programming language tells you which things are legal to write in that language. Only once a program is syntactically correct does it make sense to ask what it does, or means – that is, what its *semantics* is.

---

a We are simplifying slightly, e.g. glossing over the issue of "static semantics".

Even tiny errors, like putting a bracket in the wrong place or missing out a semi-colon, can completely invalidate your program: the computer has no ability to see what you meant, however obvious that may seem to a human. Instead it will give a *syntax error*. The good news is that these are usually easy to fix – provided you only have one at a time, which is why you should take every opportunity to check that your code is OK so far.

3.4.1 Setting Up Your Task

Usually the first thing you have to know is what the thing you are writing will be called. Often you'll be told what name to use: if so, use this *exactly* – for example, use uppercase and lowercase letters exactly as you've been given them. Otherwise, start with a name that's as descriptive as you can manage right now (even if that's just "Question1" at this stage) and make a mental note to replace it with a better name later.

Begin by writing just the skeleton of your code, so that you can check it, even before you code the real behaviour. For example, if your question was about Java, and began "Write a class MyClass that ... " you type

Java example

```
public class MyClass {
}
```

In many languages you will now have a legal program, even if you leave the inside of what you are writing empty, as in that example. In Haskell, it is useful to know about the special value undefined, which works as its name suggests, e.g.

Haskell example

```
myFunction :: String -> String
myFunction = undefined
```

We already saw undefined used in the Fizz Buzz template file. Python's pass, which we'll see in a moment, serves a similar purpose.

Check that you have the syntax correct so far, by compiling the program if you're working in a compiled language, or else by running it, following whatever language-specific instructions you have. This also checks that you know how to compile or run the program, of course. If there is an error, then the sooner you find that out, the easier it is to fix. If there are no errors, well done!

At the very beginning of learning a language, it is common to encounter a sequence of problems that nobody has warned you about, because you make mistakes that would simply never occur to someone with experience in the language. If this happens to you, don't be discouraged! Take every opportunity to check your work, and the basics will soon be second nature to you, too.

Story

Leslie is doing a course in Haskell. She reads the question which says

> Write a function max which takes two integers
> and returns the larger.

She remembers being told that when you write a function in Haskell you should first give its type, and then its definition. She also remembers – because it seemed so surprising – that the type of a function with two inputs has two arrows in it.[a] She types

```
max :: integer -> integer -> integer
```

into the environment she's been told to use, GHCi, and hits return.

Unfortunately she gets the error message

```
<interactive>:8:1: error:
  No instance for (Ord integer1) arising from a use of 'max'
  Possible fix:
    add (Ord integer1) to the context of
      an expression type signature:
        forall integer1. integer1 -> integer1 -> integer1
  In the expression: max :: integer -> integer -> integer
  In an equation for 'it': it = max :: integer -> integer -> integer
```

This doesn't mean much to her, but she doesn't panic. The first thing she realises is that she's typed integer where she should have typed Integer. Case often matters! Correcting to

```
max :: Integer -> Integer -> Integer
```

---

a This is because *strictly* speaking any Haskell function has exactly one input! Providing the "first" input produces a function capable of accepting the "second". Look up *currying* if you want to know more about this.

…unfortunately just gives her a different error message. Oh dear. What should she do?

She turns to her Haskell textbook, and finds that it talks about interacting with GHCi at the command line, but mostly seems to recommend writing code in a file, and then loading the file with :load. She tries that.

```
Prelude> :load "max.hs"
```

Next she finds

```
max.hs:1:1: error:
    The type signature for 'max' lacks an accompanying binding
      (The type signature must be given where 'max' is declared)
  |
1 | max :: Integer -> Integer -> Integer
  | ^^^
[1 of 1] Compiling Main                 ( max.hs, interpreted )
Failed, no modules loaded.
```

which she takes to mean she must define the function as well as declare its type. She adds a definition into her file:

```
max :: Integer -> Integer -> Integer
max x y
  | x >= y      = x
  | otherwise     y
```

(fortunately remembering that she's been told to use spaces, not tabs) but gets

```
Prelude> :reload

max.hs:7:1: error:
    parse error (possibly incorrect indentation or mismatched brackets)
[1 of 1] Compiling Main                 ( max.hs, interpreted )
Failed, no modules loaded.
Prelude>
```

She doesn't find this very helpful, especially since there are fewer than 7 lines in her program, so it's hard to see what the "7:1" means. Still, she doesn't panic, and eventually she notices that she has simply missed out an = sign in the last line. She puts it in, and all is well.

This wasn't a fun experience for Leslie, but at least, by checking she was doing OK after typing 4 lines, rather than 40, she made it easier for herself to sort the problem out.

Some of the named pieces of code you have to write are probably *functions*, or *methods* of a class. A *pure* function – like max in the story – is essentially a programmed version of a mathematical function, which you have probably seen illustrated as a box with one or more arrows going in, and one going out, as in Figure 3.1.

Here whatever computation goes on inside the box, to produce the output from the input, is isolated from the rest of the world: the function max operates as a *black box* with impenetrable walls. Depending on your language, though, your programmed function or method may be *impure*: that is, it may access data other than its inputs, or it may have other *effects* such as changing what is displayed on screen. You might think of such impurity as the box in Figure 3.1 having walls that are not completely solid.

As well as getting the name of your function[3] correct, you need to make sure that your code shows the correct *arguments* – that is, inputs – in the right order. If you need to give types, then the types of the arguments, and of the return value, must be correct. All this information is probably in the question: get it into your program. Sometimes this is simple. For the Fizz Buzz Python example, where

---

3 A *method* – the term used in object-oriented programming – is a kind of (impure) function, so we will often say just "function" instead of "function or method".

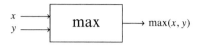

Figure 3.1. A mathematical (pure) function.

the function we have to write must take an integer argument, and does not return anything, we might write:

Python example

```
def fizz_buzz(n):
    pass
```

The word `pass` here means "do nothing", and is only there because you can't have a completely empty function body in Python. If you didn't happen to know about `pass`, you might have chosen to write `print(1)` or whatever, instead; the point is that at this stage we are not yet worrying about what the function does, just writing its casing, and as little else as possible.

If you're writing a function that has to return a value, your code will have to return something, probably of the right type, before you will be able to make it run without getting an error message. Do that now, before you think about what the function really has to do. In the Fizz Buzz Haskell example, you might replace the undefined `say` function you were given by this one:

Haskell example

```
say :: Integer -> String
say n = "1"  -- TODO
```

This is, admittedly, only a tiny advance on the version in the template, but at least, in choosing "1" as the fixed `String` value to return, we have written a function that is correct for input value

1! The "-- TODO" is a *comment*: including it makes no difference as far as the computer is concerned, but reminds you that you have not finished yet. We will discuss comments much more in Chapter 8.

Another example: if you are asked to write a public method called `calculate` that takes a `double` and returns an `int`, you could write

Java example

```java
public int calculate(double d) {
  return 0; // TODO
}
```

and again, check that your code compiles without error.

Once you've got to this stage, you've demonstrated that you know how a function or method is defined in the language, and that you have understood the type. That's something, and if you are writing for marks, getting this right may already have earned you a few.

Tip

Unlike humans, who may not even consciously notice typos in what we read, computers can be completely flummoxed by the smallest of errors. Get into the habit of checking that you haven't mis-spelled something, or put an uppercase letter where there should be a lowercase one or vice versa.

3.4.2 Making Progress Towards Fully Correct Code

Next, go on to understanding what the actual functionality you have to implement is. Again, do not feel you have to get it all correct at once. Let's look at the Fizz Buzz Python example. Suppose you think you know how to print the numbers from 1 to n: check that, before you worry about the Fizz and Buzz replacement. You might improve your function to:

Python example

```python
def fizz_buzz(n):
    for i in range(1, n):
        print(i)
```

As it happens, there is already a tiny mistake here. If you run the code now, before there are more complicated matters to distract you, you will quickly see it: Python's `range` function iterates from its lower bound to *one less than* its upper bound, so `fizz_buzz(100)` will only print the numbers from 1 to 99. We need `range(1, n+1)` instead. This is the kind of thing that is easy to miss if you only check the behaviour at the end.

Of course it is always up to you how much code you write before you check again. Inevitably, sometimes your checking will show that you have made a mistake: my recommendation is to keep your coding steps small enough that you are unlikely to have made *two* mistakes since your last check. It is much easier to find a single mistake than several that might have interacting effects. Try completing a version of the Fizz Buzz exercise in your language now.

Skeletons and specifications

Why does it help to work from the outside in? Because the outside is usually crucial to the *specification* of what you have to do. For example, when writing a function, the most important thing to understand is what information goes *in* – the arguments, and their types – and what information must come *out* – the return value, and its type, plus any other effects your function must have. Get the relationship between those right, and you've done it. The outside world – the *clients* of your function – will not care how you implemented the function, provided that when they give suitable arguments they get a suitable result. This is *abstraction*, and it's a key part of programming. We'll return to this idea in Chapter 10.

As you bring your program closer to completion, save a version every time you have got another small thing working. Ideally, do this by checking your code into a version control system (see Chapter 6), but an alternative is to save copies of your program file, with informative names to remind you which version is which. That way you can try things out, secure in the knowledge that if something goes wrong you haven't lost much – you can go back to a recent working state.

3.5 What to Do If You Get Confused

Sometimes you may find you can get the skeleton of your code written easily enough, but you feel stumped when it comes to going on from there. Perhaps the instructions are confusing, or perhaps you understand what they mean but have no idea how to fulfil them.

One thing I like to do if I am outside my comfort zone is to make notes on my progress. I often do this by having a file called notes.txt in the same directory where I am writing the program, and writing notes to myself in this as I go. What I write depends on what it is about the task that seems tricky. Faced with a large-scale problem where I understand what I have to do but am not sure how best to write a program to do it, I might write *design notes*, planning out the structure of the code or an *algorithm* (computational recipe) I will use. However, generally – and especially for student beginners – my experience is that it usually works better to develop the program itself iteratively, testing as you go and improving the structure of the program as your understanding of the problem and solution deepens. In `notes.txt` I more often describe my current state of understanding. For example, I might write:

Notes

Function foo[a] is supposed to do something with strings ...
I don't understand the explanation in general ... but at least
if it gets a string with only one letter in, it should return True if
the letter is a vowel and False otherwise.

---

a Why foo? See the box at the end of this chapter.

Even if I'm wrong about that – I've misinterpreted the question – the fact of typing it prompts me to think about what I do and don't understand, and gives me a record of where I got to and what I was assuming at the time, which may be useful later.

When confusion threatens, it often helps to make your hypotheses explicit and test them. For example, if you have the feeling that your program works OK on simple inputs but has some problem that's affecting more complicated inputs, ask yourself what exactly you mean by "simple inputs". Write it down:

Notes

Hypothesis: the program always works correctly on strings with
just one character.

Then test your hypothesis with some specific one-character strings. Include some you think might be tricky, such as a space or punctuation character. Either your program does always behave correctly on one-character strings, in which case you can confidently go on to sorting out the bigger issue, or it doesn't. If it doesn't, you can now work on the problem of making your program do the right thing on one-character strings, which is easier to think about than making it do the right thing on all strings. Either way, you win.

> **Tip**
>
> Always work on the easiest problem first.

Once you've solved part of the problem, even a tiny trivial part, you're in a position to ask yourself: "is my program perfect yet?". If not, how do you know? Specifically? Answering that gives you the next small problem to work on, and so on.

When you find a case where the program doesn't work, make sure you have a note of what the case is, what your program should do, and what it actually does. Writing automated tests, as discussed in Chapter 7, is a really good way to keep track of this, but even if you're not doing that yet, making notes – both of what works and of what doesn't yet – can help. Especially when you're very tired, it's remarkably easy to get yourself into a state where you think a certain thing used to work, but you're not sure; or you may slip into trying to write a program that isn't the one you want at all.

Ideally, following this process round a few loops gets you unconfused, to the point where you've finished your problem. If not, you can probably at least get yourself into one of two situations:

1. There is something specific that you do not understand about what the program is supposed to do. Cut it down to the simplest possible case you're not sure about. If you can, analyse what it is you don't understand. Are you unsure whether a certain input is allowed at all? Or are there two behaviours that might be expected under particular circumstances, and you're not sure which is right? Or what? Reread the problem statement with that specific question in mind. If it's still not clear, it's probably time to ask someone else.

2. There is some specific problem with your program: it gives you an error message, or it does not behave the way you expect on some input. That is, it contains a *bug*. This is the topic of Chapter 9.

Either way, analysing your problem is a big step towards solving it. Try to avoid simply asking to see a solution: instead, asking for the precise bit of help that will let you complete your own solution will serve you better in the long run, and be much more satisfying.

Foo, bar, baz, mung, froboz

These are names commonly used to stand in place of the actual names of functions, variables, etc. in conversation, when the actual names are not important, or not yet decided. For example, if you are discussing how function calling works, you might say, "Suppose a function foo calls a function bar ...": here what you are about to say applies when any function calls any other function, but you need some names for them, so that you can use the names to refer to the functions later. Such names are sometimes called *metasyntactic*. By long tradition, foo and bar are the first two that programmers call upon; these names are probably a corruption of the military slang abbreviation FUBAR, standing for F***ed Up Beyond All Recognition. After that, there are several divergent traditions about what names to use (and froboz is often spelled frobozz).

Recognising and using the usual metasyntactic variable names may help you to give the impression of having more experience than you do! However, using them as actual names in your program is generally a bad idea – in Chapter 8 we will discuss why it is important to choose names that are meaningful.

4

How to Understand Your Language

In Chapter 14 we'll talk about how to choose an appropriate programming language for a given task. In this chapter, though, we'll start with the assumption that you don't have a choice – you have to learn a language chosen by someone else. What do you nevertheless need to understand about *the landscape of all programming languages*, and how your language fits into it?

You may object that that's not what the title of this chapter is about: isn't understanding your language just learning to understand, and write, programs in it? Well: no, not only that. It's also useful to understand something about the decisions that were taken in designing it: how, and why, it differs from other languages. If someone else chose this language for you to learn, why did they choose this one? Why will learning this language, in particular, be valuable to you?

That said, people learn in different ways, and some people may wish to skip this chapter for now. Feel free – but do come back to it later.

If you're still here, questions you might ask (ask your instructor, ask your favourite search engine) include:

• What kind of task was this language developed for? When, and by whom?
• Who uses it now, and for what?
• What kind of community is there of people who use this language? Where do they hang out online?
• Is your language compiled or interpreted?
• What kind of type discipline does it impose?

- What high-level structure do programs in your language have?
- What conventions do people obey? You'd be surprised how important things like how words are capitalised can be, in terms of helping experts in the language quickly understand your program, and in terms of making you look like someone who knows the language! There are also conventions about many other things, from how long parts of the program tend to get before an expert would decide to split them up, to which libraries are used.

Let's discuss some of these questions. We'll start from the more concrete questions, and come to the more sociological ones later.

4.1 Compilation or Interpretation

A question which can seem silly to people who already know the answer – and to which, therefore, they may forget to tell you the answer – is: once I have written my program, how do I get it to run? There are two main answers:

1. You just run it.
2. You compile it, then run it.

This is a simplification, although it's a useful one because the presence or absence of a compilation activity tends to make a big difference to how it feels to program in a language. Let us give the simplified explanation first, before addressing the ways in which it's an over-simplification.

"You just run it" applies to languages, for example Python, JavaScript (NB nothing to do with Java, despite the similar name!), PHP and Perl, which are *interpreted*. That means that there is some other program, called an interpreter, which reads your program and does what it says. If there is a problem somewhere in your program which means that part of the program cannot be interpreted, the interpreter will give some kind of error message, and stop, when it gets to that part. However, by then it may already have run the earlier parts of the program.

"You compile it, then run it" applies to languages, for example Java, Haskell and all variants of C (C++, C$^\sharp$, Objective-C, etc.), which are *compiled*. That means that there is some other program, called a compiler, which reads your program and translates it into a more primitive form. Some kinds of error in your program can be detected in the process of compilation. If no such errors are discovered, then you end up with a compiled program, saved as a separate file, which you can then run, as above. Because some of the work has been done by the compiler, the compiled program usually runs faster than an interpreted program with the same functionality. What is often more important is that, because the compiler has checked for certain kinds of error, you get a guarantee: if your program compiles correctly, then you can be sure that that kind of error is absent. The main kind of error-checking the compiler does is called *type-checking*: we will have more to say about types in Section 4.2.

Story

In 1978, Robin Milner published a theorem about the core of the programming language he defined, which is called ML; this language has influenced Haskell and many later programming languages. The theorem can be summarised as "well-typed programs cannot 'go wrong'". That is, he *proved* that if the compiler accepted your program, then your program was definitely free of certain kinds of error. When I first worked with ML, some of my colleagues used to describe it as "the language of pure thought" and say that if your program compiled, there was no need to test it: it was certainly correct! Unfortunately this is an exaggeration: but still, it is remarkably useful to have a compiler that is good at noticing when you have made a mistake, even if it can be frustrating to be told so.

To find out exactly how you get from having a file containing a program in your language, to the result of running the program, you need a basic tutorial in the language. If you don't already have one, search for one now, using the searches mentioned in Chapter 3:

---

 install *your_language*

---

 getting started *your_language*

In Python, for example, you can save your program in a file called myprogram.py, and then run it by typing

```
python myprogram.py
```

at a command line. In Java, you define a class called `MyProgram` in a file called MyProgram.java, and then compile and run the program by typing first

```
javac MyProgram.java
```

to compile it, and then

```
java MyProgram
```

to run it.

Sometimes the lines between interpreted and compiled languages get blurred: I admitted to an over-simplification. Strictly speaking, whether a language is compiled or interpreted is a property of the *implementation* of the language, not of the language itself. Even in languages which are usually interpreted, like Python, it is often possible to compile a program into a form (a .pyc file) which can be run faster than the original and which has been checked for certain kinds of problem. And even languages which are compiled, like Haskell, can sometimes be used in interactive situations (e.g. the Haskell REPL) which feel very much like interpretation. Moreover, in some languages, like C and C++, another stage, called *linking*, is made explicit. This connects the compiled program with any libraries that must be available before it can be run. All programs have to get connected to the libraries they depend on at some stage, of course, but this isn't always something the programmer has to do deliberately. For example, in Java, linking is done by the Java Virtual Machine when the class is loaded: that is, it's part of what the run command, `java MyProgram`, causes to happen.

4.2 Types

If you have ever been reminded to "show the units" in your answer to a problem in a mathematics or science class, you have met types. Arguably, if you've ever watched a baby using a shape-sorter, you have, too! The *type* of a value in a program tells you something about what you can legitimately do with it. What do you need to know about a value in order to know that it makes sense to use it in a particular context?

Terminology: Type-checking

Type-checking is the process of checking that the shapes of the pieces of a program fit together properly: for example, that a function that has been designed to accept only integers is never given strings as its input. If this is done as part of compilation, it is called *static type-checking*; if it is done at run-time, it is called *dynamic type-checking*. Many languages use a mixture of static and dynamic type-checking.

Almost every programming language has types of *integers* and *strings*, for example. You'll be familiar with integers from school mathematics; "string" is the computer science term for a piece of text, or sequence of characters. By long tradition, the first string we experiment with is "Hello, World!". A *Hello World program* in a language is a program which prints out "Hello, World!" when you run it. Our program will do slightly more.

Python example

```
x = 5
y = 2
z = "Hello, World!"
print(x)
print(y)
print(z)
print(x/y)
print(x/z)
```

No types are given explicitly in this program, but they are there: if you try running it, you will get an error at the last line, something like

```
TypeError: unsupported operand type(s) for /:
'int' and 'str'
```

Once you think about what the program is doing on that line, this is easy to understand, whether or not you "speak" Python. Variables x and y hold integers; variable z holds a string. We don't have to say that: the language's *type inference* works it out. Any of x, y and z can be printed. It makes sense to divide an integer by an integer (even though, note, the result is not an integer any longer). However, it does not make sense to divide an integer by a string. The interpreter does not even try: instead, it tells you that you have got something wrong.

Languages differ in how they treat information about the types of values. If we write the same program in Java, it looks like this:

Java example

```
int x = 5;
int y = 2;
String z = "Hello, World!";
System.out.println(x);
System.out.println(y);
System.out.println(z);
System.out.println(x/y);
System.out.println(x/z);
```

(as usual, we omit the lines that show this code placed inside a method inside a class). This is very similar to the Python example: compiling it will give an error at the final line, because you can't divide an integer by a string. Whereas in the Python case, the earlier, unproblematic print statements were carried out before the interpreter encountered the nonsensical instruction to print x/z, in the Java case, since compilation does not succeed, none of the instructions can be carried out until the problem is fixed and the program is recompiled.

Apart from the System.out.println verbiage, the biggest difference between this version and the Python one is that here we have to give the types of the variables x, y, z in the program text. (There is still some type inference going on, though: for example, we do not have to say what type the expression x/y has. By the way, if you're learning Java: what type *does* it have? Removing the last line and wrapping this code in a method in a class, compile and run it. Did it print what you expected?)

In Haskell, it is rather unidiomatic[1] to write anything of the sort, but we can, if we insist:

---

1 That is, the code does not abide by the conventions usually followed by Haskell experts, e.g. including types for top-level functions.

Haskell example

```
f _ =
  do print x
     print y
     print z
     print (x/y)
     print (x/z)
  where x = 5
        y = 2
        z = "Hello,_World!"
```

As with Java, we won't be able to compile this – let alone invoke function f to run the code – until we get rid of the nonsensical line about x/z. Just as in the Python example, we did not have to write any types; they are inferred. Here, however, type inference is done as part of the compilation phase. We cannot execute any of the program until the types of all of it make sense.

Tip

If you are learning a language other than Python, Java or Haskell, try writing a version of this program in your language now.

We cannot really think without types: even programs written in apparently untyped languages have implicit type information. Even if, in your language, you are not forced to write down information about what you expect types to be, it is wise to clarify your expectations in your own head. Sometimes it is useful to write them down, even if you don't have to: it can help you, and other readers of your program, understand what's going on. One of the ways in which our Haskell example was unusual was that it did not specify the type of function f.

All the examples above used built-in types for strings and integers. All major languages have these types built in. To write real programs you also have to be able to define your own types, and languages differ in how you do that.

All the examples also demonstrated *polymorphism*: that is, we could use the same function to print things of several different types. Printing is the commonest situation where language designers feel obliged to provide polymorphism. Whether, and how, you can write your own polymorphic functions – that is, functions that work on arguments of several different types – is another axis on which programming languages differ. Indeed, it is a particularly interesting one, as there are different kinds of polymorphism. Try searching

 polymorphism *your_language*

if you want to know more about this.

4.3 Structure

In a beginners' programming course, the way in which large programs are structured may be invisible to you. You will probably only write small programs to start with; you may, perhaps, write only a few lines of code, and be told where to put them.

All serious programs, though, have to have structure. They have to be split up into parts, so that teams of people can work on different parts of the program without getting in one another's way. The structure of a program is what makes it possible to make a change to a program, without having to understand everything about the entire program. This helps with finding and fixing bugs quickly and confidently, for example.

We mentioned functions, as black box machines transforming input into output, in Chapter 3. When you define a function (or method, or procedure) in your programming language, you are structuring the program so that the lines of code that define what this machine does (the *body* of the function) are together. While this section of code may not be completely self-contained – it may depend on other parts of the program, e.g. by calling other functions – the aim is that a reader can understand what the function will do, just by reading its body code. This sounds very basic, but it could not always be taken for granted – search

---

 goto considered harmful

---

if you would like to read about the early history of structure in programs.

An intimately related issue is the scope of names.

> **Terminology: Scope**
>
> Many things in programs – variables, functions and classes, for example – are given names. The *scope* of a name for a thing means where, in the program text, the name can be used to refer to the thing. If the name can be used anywhere in the program, it is said to have global scope.

Global scope may sound convenient, but there is an important disadvantage: if you need to understand the role this named thing plays – e.g. to work out whether a change you have in mind will break anything – you have to read the whole program. Therefore, programming languages allow named things to have smaller scopes. For example, a variable might be local to a function, so that it can only be referred to inside that function's definition. The details are subtle and vary between languages: if you want to know more, try searching

 scope *your_language*

Your language may provide classes, modules, packages, or several of these. Very likely these higher-level structures will be used to provide *libraries* which make it easier for you to write programs.

> **Terminology: Library**
>
> A software *library* provides functionality designed to be used in many other programs. A *standard library* for a language is one that is maintained along with the basic software implementing the language, and distributed with it, so that it is always available to someone programming in the language.

Standard libraries provide things which are frequently needed, such as code for finding a pattern in a string, collections that can be sorted efficiently, user interface components, etc. If your language has a standard library, becoming familiar with it is an integral part of learning to program well in the language.

Many libraries, and much of the other software implementing major programming languages, are open-source.

> **Terminology: Open-source**
>
> Software is *open-source* when it is made available under licensing conditions that allow anyone to view the source code, modify it, and redistribute their modified version. Typically, there are conditions, such as that the modified software must itself be made available with the same licence.

For you as a beginning programmer, the immediate advantages of using open-source software are that it is usually free,[2] and that you can, if you wish, look at the source code to learn from it. Later you may wish to contribute to an open-source project: see Chapter 15.

4.4 History, Community and Motivation

How old is your language? Who designed it? What is it used for? If you are doing a beginners' programming course, one question is: are you using a language that is used mostly for teaching, or one that is also widely used by professional developers? The languages we discuss most in this book are used in both settings, but you may have come across educational languages such as Scratch, or some language for turtle graphics based on Logo; you may now be learning Alice. Similar questions apply to the tooling you are using: for example, you might be using the education-focused IDE BlueJ, for Java. The lines between categories do get blurred, and successful languages outgrow their niches: for example BASIC, the name of a language designed in the early 1960s, stands for Beginner's All-purpose Symbolic Instruction Code, but its Visual Basic dialect went on to be very widely used by experts as well as beginners.

Most likely, your language is used by some professional developers. To do what? Reading its Wikipedia page, or searching

 who uses *your_language*

will find you some information (and possibly some examples of the *language wars*). In the process, you may find out something about the *community* surrounding your language. Perhaps your language is a *scripting language*, often used for automating sequences of tasks that would otherwise have to be done manually by humans.

---

2 In the sense that you do not pay money for it: you might like to look up the different meanings of "free software".

These are interpreted languages: Python is usually considered a scripting language, although these days it is also used for many other purposes. Or perhaps your language is mostly used for web services, or in AI, or data science, or embedded programming, or statistics. Which websites have the most useful bodies of questions and answers about it? Bookmark them!

4.5 Paradigms

We have left until last something which comparative discussions of programming languages sometimes take first. Traditionally, programming languages have been divided into groups according to the main way in which people writing in those languages tend to think – that is, according to *paradigm*. The four main paradigms usually identified are:

- Imperative. The program orders the computer to do one thing, then another thing. Data is stored in the form of *mutable state*, i.e. variables which have values that can be changed. Example language: C.
- Object-oriented. The program is organised in terms of objects. Each object wraps up (*encapsulates*) some data, and can respond to certain requests (*messages*), thereby fulfilling some responsibilities. Example language: Java.
- Functional. The programmer thinks of functions not just as bits of code, but as concrete things in their own right – as data – which can be passed around the program. For example, a function can be passed as an argument to another function, just as an integer might be. (People sometimes say functions are "first-class citizens".) Mutable state is avoided. Example language: Haskell.
- Logic. Writing a program involves specifying facts, and rules about how facts follow from other facts, and then asking a question. Example language: Prolog.

However, real life is nothing like as neat as this, and some people argue that it isn't useful to think in terms of paradigms. As you program in more than one language, you naturally import your favourite ways of thinking – influenced by your past programming experience – into each language you adopt. Some languages – Python is an example, in fact – have a mixture of features that makes them hard to classify. And sometimes a language that begins neatly in one paradigm may change, over time, to make it easier to program in a style that began elsewhere. For example, Java version 8 introduced new features that made it more practical to program in a functional style.

Does this mean you can just pick your favourite way to program and then program that way in any language? To some extent you *can*, but it's unlikely to be the best approach. For example, you can write a C program in a functional style, but, because C doesn't support functional programming very well, your program is not likely to be *good*. It will be all too easy to make mistakes, and all too hard for any reader (including you, later) to understand the program. Try to go with the grain of your chosen language (whether or not it was chosen by you): learn from the way experts in that language typically write. That is, learn to write *idiomatically* in your language. At the same time, be alert to the good features of different programming styles you come across, and be ready to make use of them *where appropriate*.

Tip

To help you get a feel for what is considered good, idiomatic code in your language, find a fairly large, highly reputable body of code. Look at it and remember to come back to it at intervals as you learn the language. Don't worry if you can't understand it in detail at this stage. Consult it if you ever wonder about such things as "how long should a function be?", "how should I capitalise the name of a type?", etc.

Standard libraries, for example, are written by experts who expect their code to be inspected by many other experts, so they tend to be good – though not especially beginner-friendly – code.

- Java: the OpenJDK version of the Java Development Kit has source code at http://hg.openjdk.java.net/jdk/jdk/. Look for the "browse" entry in the left-hand menu.
- Haskell: if you use Hoogle (https://hoogle.haskell.org/) to look up a function, there is a link to its source code to the right of its name.
- Python: if you use the documentation available from https://docs.python.org/3/library/ for the standard library, you will see links to source code near the top of most pages.

Your language-specific book or documentation should provide plenty of examples of simpler code.

5

How to Use the Best Tools

In the earliest days of computing, programs took the form of punched cards that had to be fed into a computer, and programming was slow work. Naturally, the programmers, who understood the power of computers, wanted computers to help make the work of programming easier, faster and more reliable. These days, there is a wide – and constantly changing – assortment of tools to support the software development process. Some tools – e.g. compilers – perform a clearly delineated task; others, especially *integrated development environments*, bring together many capabilities and present a uniform interface to them. Learning to make good use of tools is an important part of learning to write good programs.

Programming courses vary a lot in how much instruction they give on tool use. You may be told precisely what to use and how, or you may get a suggestion of what tool to use but be left to find out about its capabilities yourself, or you may be completely on your own. Naturally, to whatever extent learning to use a particular tool is part of your course, you need to do that; but it is also useful to have a broader view of what is available. When you program outside or beyond your course, you may be able to choose the tools you prefer. If you plan a career in software development, you will need to be able to adapt to whatever tool set is in use in the organisation where you work. Widening your experience is worthwhile, both to let you make good choices when you can, and to give you the skills to fit in when you must.

As we shall see in the rest of the book, appropriate tools can help you throughout the process of developing software: from starting a new programming project, through editing, compiling, running, testing, debugging and improving your program. In the rest of this chapter, we will discuss the ways in which tools can support the basic *writing* of a program. On the way, we will discuss the factors that may guide you in choosing a tool.

5.1 Using the Most Basic Tools

Until now, we have assumed you are using a text editor to write your program, and then compiling and running the program from the operating system's command line. This has the advantage that it makes it easy to understand which tool does what task – by contrast, the more sophisticated tools can sometimes be mystifying. It is a good idea to be *able* to write, compile, test and run your program using nothing more complex than a plain text editor – a *dumb editor*, one that does not have any special features for supporting programming – and a command line, even if you don't choose to work that way day-to-day.

Powerful, extensible text editors, such as Emacs and Atom, often have extensions to let them support programming in various languages. For example, in Emacs you should edit a Python program using the editor in *python mode*, and provided that you use the standard extension .py for your Python files, you will probably find that the editor enters this mode automatically. The most obvious thing you will notice is that you get automatic *syntax highlighting*, which gives a visual difference between, for example, keywords in the language, such as if, and variable names that you chose. Note that, even though the visual effects can look similar to what you might produce in a word processor, here the editor *computes* what effects to use where. No instructions about these visual effects are stored in the program file, which is still just plain text that you can open in any text editor.

Editor modes, which can be quite simple or very powerful, are easier for people to write than specialist development tools, so they are typically available even for less common programming languages. Moreover, some people prefer being able to run their whole lives from one program. I, for example, use Emacs for managing my mail, writing my papers, organising my files, and most of my day-to-day programming – though for Java, I find it worthwhile to switch out of Emacs to a specialist IDE.

5.2 What Is an IDE?

In Chapter 3 we introduced the term *integrated development environment* as "an application that supports the whole process of developing a program". This is a bit vague, and indeed, IDEs differ in their capabilities. You may expect an IDE to support at least writing, compiling (if that's relevant to your language), running, testing (Chapter 7), and debugging (Chapter 9) your program.

Typically the IDE presents you with a graphical front-end, behind which are the same tools you could use from the command line: for example, the IDE might have a menu item for testing your program, which, behind the scenes, invokes a testing tool you could also choose to invoke directly. However, there are a number of benefits to the integration of many individual tools in one application.

- They can be presented to you in a consistent, easy-to-use way; you can invoke them from menus instead of having to remember individual tool names. Good interface design can also make it easy for you to discover capabilities by exploring the interface.
- The IDE can keep track of your workflow – for example, if you try to run a program which you have edited since you last saved it, the IDE will probably ask you whether you want to save your work first.
- The IDE can provide you with intelligent links between the output of one tool and what you are likely to want to do next. For example, if compiling your program reveals that there is an error on line 13, clicking on the error message may position the IDE's editor at line 13.
- The IDE will have a notion of *project*: that is, of a collection of files that go to make up a complete program. To begin with, your programs may just be single files, and the notion of project will not seem useful. Later, though, a project might include multiple

files of code, tests, some resources that the program needs at run-time (such as images for use in the program's user interface), a record of what external libraries the program needs, a *build file* which specifies dependencies between the files and how they are combined into running software, etc. The IDE's ability to help manage these files and their dependencies can then be very helpful.

You can simply use an IDE as a text editor, and then compile and run your program using menu items.

Tip

Make sure you know the keyboard shortcut for saving your program, so that you don't have to go to a menu every time.

More generally, think about how to use the tool in a way which is efficient and comfortable for you. Programming, especially for many hours a day, can lead to repetitive strain injury (RSI); simple steps like knowing the keyboard shortcuts, for the things you do most often, can help a lot.

Here are some of the most useful capabilities that an IDE will probably offer you, besides basic editing.

Offering Constructive Criticism You may find that the way the IDE points out mistakes you have made in your program is more helpful than the way the compiler or interpreter does so: for one thing, it will at least try to give you a visual indication of where in your program the error is.

For example, if you edit Java code using Eclipse, and you make a syntax error, you will see a red cross in the left margin and a red squiggly line under part of your code. (Eclipse actually compiles your code *incrementally*, which is why it can show you errors almost immediately after you make them.)

I recommend that whenever you see such an error indicator, you fix the problem immediately. Under no circumstances should you use the IDE's settings to turn off the error indicators, as one student I encountered did: the errors are still there, even if you make the red marks go away!

The tool may offer *quick fixes*: that is, if you hover over or click on an error indicator, there may be a menu of changes that may fix the error, which the tool can then apply automatically. These are worth considering, although the tool is not all that intelligent, and the right thing to do may not be one of the suggestions.

Keeping Your Work Neat A capability the IDE will offer, that beginners often under-value, is to help lay out your code consistently. You will probably find that you can select a region of code and choose a menu item called something like Format, to make lines of code line up where they should, and so on. We will discuss this, and why it is important, in Chapter 8. The very short version is that it makes your code easier to read, and makes you more likely to notice when what you wrote is not what you intended.

Saving You Typing More of a mixed blessing is the IDE's ability to save you typing parts of your code, for example by auto-completing long function names, or by telling you what pieces of syntax make sense to put next in a given context.

Terminology: Autocompletion

Autocompletion – sometimes called *code completion* or *content assist* – is when the IDE saves you typing. For example, if you have typed enough of a function name that there is only one function you could mean, the IDE may be able to insert the rest. Or, it may pop up a menu for you to choose between possible functions. Try hitting the TAB key, or Ctrl and the space bar together, and see if anything useful happens. Searching

 autocomplete *your_IDE*

will give you fuller information about what's available.

Autocompletion can be convenient, and it may even encourage you to write better code: as we shall discuss in Chapter 8, you should avoid using cryptic abbreviations as names in your program, and the temptation to do that is lessened when autocompletion helps you use a better, longer name without incurring more keystrokes.

The downside is that, if you habitually rely on autocompletion to insert names from a standard library, or other bits of program text, you may not internalise them. Then you may find yourself unexpectedly stuck when, for some reason, you have to program using a dumb editor. Be aware.

5.3 Looking Forward

To begin with, you may be content to use just the most basic features of a tool that has been recommended to you. It is common, however, to find that an IDE you have been using for years has features that would have been fantastically useful to you, if only you had known they existed. For example, IDEs often integrate with various build systems, with version control systems (Chapter 6), and with public repositories like GitHub. When you have time, see if the tool has a tutorial, perhaps accessible via a Help menu, that may tell you about such things.

Once you're feeling quite confident with programming, experimenting with different IDEs can be worthwhile; you may well find one you prefer to the one your programming course told you to use, either because it has extra features that you value, or because you find it more usable. Try searching

 best ide *your_language*

and browsing reviews, to decide what to try. Some common IDEs today that are used both in teaching contexts and by professional developers are Eclipse, IntelliJ IDEA and NetBeans, which are available on many platforms, and Visual Studio (Microsoft and Apple operating systems). There are many others, free and commercial, including some written specifically to help students (e.g. BlueJ for Java). The choice is also dependent on what programming language you're working in. Java is by far the best supported by IDEs.

The most popular IDEs, such as Eclipse, also support ecosystems of *plug-ins*: that is, they have an extension mechanism which lets people other than the original developers of the IDE extend the IDE's capabilities in whatever direction they desire – from imposing custom layout styles to integrating with tools for modelling and verification. This is usually not a job for a beginning programmer, but if you ever wish your IDE did something that it does not do, remember that, in a year or two's time when you're looking for an interesting project . . .

6

How to Make Sure You Don't Lose Your Program

Have you ever had the experience of working on something for a significant length of time, and then losing it entirely when a program crashed or a connection was lost? Or simply because you closed a window you shouldn't have closed? Or because you thought you didn't need a certain chunk of it, and deleted it, only to realise a moment later that you did need it? Whether we're talking about an essay, your latest social media post or a program, it's really annoying. Fortunately, it's largely avoidable.

Making sure you don't lose your program, or valuable sections of it, is partly a matter of using the right tools, and partly a matter of developing habits that will save you from your own mistakes. People often have strong views on the right way to do it, but in truth, there are many ways that work, each with its own pros and cons.

The key tool is, of course, the one you're using to write the program. Whether that's an editor or an integrated development environment (see Chapter 5), make sure you understand what it can do for you.

6.1 Immediate Recovery: Undo

The most important facility that helps you recover, immediately, from momentary mistakes, is the *undo* feature. Most of the tools you'd consider these days have "infinite" undo – that is, you can undo not just your last edit, but the one before that and so on, even back to the state the file was in when you loaded it into the editor. They typically have a corresponding *redo* feature, for when you accidentally undo too far. These can be extremely useful, but they can also be a little confusing, especially when you are feeling stressed because you've realised you messed something up.

> **Tip**
>
> Experiment with the undo and redo features of your editor before you actually need them.

If it turns out you're using a tool that has no undo/redo facility, or only has one level, i.e. you can only undo the last edit … seriously consider switching to another tool, if you can. If you don't have a choice, pay even more attention to the rest of this chapter.

6.2 Basic Disaster Recovery: Files

Computers have primary storage, usually called *memory*, and secondary storage, usually *disk*. When you open a program file in your editor, relevant data from disk is copied into memory. As you program, what you see on the screen in front of you is the state of what's in memory. It can be different from what's on disk, because as you work on the program, you change the state of the copy that is in memory, but not the state of the copy that is on disk. When you save the file, the version in memory replaces the version on disk, so that the two become the same again. Since you are gradually improving your program, this is generally a good thing, and I suggested earlier that you train your fingers into saving often.

However, if you find yourself with a disastrously broken version of your program in front of you – for example, perhaps you just accidentally deleted a huge chunk – the very last thing you want to do is to have this version replace what is on disk, so at this moment, do not save! Think carefully. Can you use undo to get back to a good state? If so, do so. Or, did you save recently, so that you are confident that the version on disk is pretty close to what you want? In that case, close your file *without* saving, and reopen it from disk.

If it is a long time since you saved the file to disk, though, using the version on disk may not help: you may have done a lot of work that is not recorded in either version. At this point it helps to know about an often-overlooked but occasionally useful feature that most tools have: autosaving. That is, every few minutes or after a certain number of key strokes, they save a version of your program, not onto the file you got it from (saving to that is under your explicit control) but somewhere else. In the days when tools were less reliable than they are now, this feature was introduced to guard against the editor crashing. These days, it's more likely to be useful when you make a mistake. See what your tool does or can do, either by searching

 autosave *your_toolname*

or by browsing your filespace. You may find that in the same place where your program file lives, there is another file with a variant of its name which is the autosaved file, or you may find that your tool uses a different directory or folder to store its autosaved files in.

If you do something wrong in a file and want to go back to an earlier version, but for some reason you can't do so using undo, try this:

1. Take your hands off the keyboard and mouse. Doing nothing is not going to make matters worse: anything you do without thinking it through might. Especially, saving the current, wrong, version of your file may destroy useful information on disk, so don't do that!
2. Think: might the current version on disk be at least a bit useful? Or, given what you know about your tool, might there be a useful autosaved version of the file?

3. Use a file browsing application to go and see. If you find a file you think might be useful, make a copy of it with a new name, so that your tool will not automatically overwrite it.
4. Once you're sure you've got copies of each version of the file that might be useful, you can go back to your tool, save whatever needs saving, look at all the file versions, and merge them appropriately.
5. You can do the merging by hand, just copying and pasting useful bits of the file, or you can use a comparison and merge facility from your tool or elsewhere – I like Emacs' `ediff` command for this.

6.3 Avoiding Disaster: Saving Versions

When you are solving a programming problem, you typically do so in many small stages, solving gradually more of the problem. Sometimes your attempt at the next stage fails, and you may even break something that was working before. You can save yourself the frustration of "going backwards" in this way, by developing a reliable "ratchet" technique that means you can always return to the *best* state you have reached so far.

The most basic way to do this is to save a copy of your program file each time you reach a new high point. Give your copy a name that reminds you how far you've got, and then go back to editing the copy of the file with the real name.

Story

Jennifer is doing an exercise in many parts, all of which involve improving file `customer.hs`. She edits `customer.hs` until she has Part A of the question done to her satisfaction. Before starting Part B, she saves a copy with the new name `customerPartADone.hs`. (She makes it a read-only file, having previously made the mistake of accidentally carrying on editing in the file that was supposed to be a safe copy.) Then she goes back to editing `customer.hs` to work on Part B. Once that's done, she saves the new version as `customerPartsAandBDone.hs`, and goes back to editing `customer.hs`, and so on. If she got totally confused while working on Part C, she knows she could always discard her unsuccessful work on Part C, copy `customerPartsAandBDone.hs` to `customer.hs`, and start Part C again. As it happens, she never does get so confused this time, but she feels safer knowing that the saved versions are there.

The more confidence you can arrange to have in the correctness of your saved versions, the more useful they will be to you. At a minimum, you should check that your editor and the compiler don't find any errors in them (apart, perhaps, from errors that simply show you haven't solved the whole problem yet – though see Chapter 3 for how to minimise those by getting to compiling code as soon as possible by writing the outsides first).

It's also a good idea to test your program before you save each version – see Chapter 7 for more on this.

6.4 Automating the Process: Using a Version Control System

Once you get into the habit of saving versions of your file, like this, you will quickly realise that it would be helpful to have some tool support for the process. This is the job of a *version control system*. Even a simple, single-user version control system will let you:

* *check in* a new version whenever you wish;
* associate comments with the new version, e.g. to record what this version achieves;

- retrieve a history of all the versions you've checked in, with their comments (particularly useful if you go back to a program you were working on a while ago);
- recover any past version you want.

Most of the systems you'll come across these days have many more features than these. For example, they keep track of a related family of files, and let you check them all in together – this becomes crucial when you work on systems with large numbers of files. They usually have facilities to let teams of people work together on large systems, with some hope of not interfering with one another's changes. The use of such facilities is beyond the scope of this book, though. Summarising very briefly, version control systems have been through three generations:

- First generation: simple single-user systems. The only one you are likely to come across these days is RCS, which is installed on most Unix systems. It is so ancient that people may laugh if you tell them that is what you are using, but it does everything you need as a beginner!
- Second generation: more complex systems that support multiple users, all working with the same files that are stored in a single central repository. SVN, short for Subversion, is the most used today. It is available on all the operating systems you are likely to use. You can use it from the command-line, or you might prefer to interact with it via a client that offers a graphical interface (such as TortoiseSVN on Windows, or Versions on a Mac). Command-line use may be a little less intuitive to start with, but may make it easier to transfer your understanding from one platform to another.
- Third generation: distributed systems, allowing each user to have their own repository so that they can continue to work even when they are not all connected to the internet. Git is the best known, and is available on all major platforms; again there is a command-line interface and a choice of graphical clients. Familiarity with Git will help you if you want to make use of

open-source projects stored on GitHub, which is a Git-based hosting service – you can even store your own code there (more on this in Section 6.6).

If you are using an IDE (Chapter 5) you are likely to find that it has version control, based on SVN or Git, integrated in it: using this is likely to be easier than using a standalone version control client.

Tip

While you just want a version control system for your course exercises, simple beats full-featured; on the other hand, life is a lot easier if someone nearby is familiar with the system you choose to use, so consider asking around and going with what other people use.

  Whatever you use, go through a tutorial carefully, and try out the tool with some dummy files, before you trust it with your important files. Searching for

 name_of_version_control_system tutorial

will find you one.

6.5 Managing Code that Is Not in Use

It'll often happen that you write a section of code, and then discover you don't want it in your program, for example because you think of a better way to solve the problem. Particularly when you're a beginner, it can also happen that your code doesn't do what you think it should do, and you don't quite understand why, and you decide to implement the functionality a different way instead. What do you do with the code now it's no longer useful? You could just delete it, or you could comment it out.

Terminology: Commenting out

To *comment out* code is to hide it from the compiler and interpreter, while leaving it in the program for a human reader.

Languages typically have a character, or character sequence, which tells the compiler or interpreter "ignore the rest of this line". (The main purpose of the syntax is, of course, to allow you to write natural language comments, which we'll discuss in Chapter 8.) In Java, C, and many other languages the character syntax is `//`; in Python, Perl, and various others it's `#`; in Haskell it's `--`; etc. You can just type the comment characters at the beginning of each line you want to comment out, but that gets tedious fast if you want to comment out more than a line or two. There are two alternatives.

1. In an IDE, you can typically select a block of code, and then use a menu item or key combination that acts on the selection to insert the comment character at the beginning of every line in the block. Selecting a commented block to *uncomment* by removing the comment characters works similarly. The IDE will typically use a different font or colour to display commented-out lines, so that they are easily distinguished from active lines of code, too. This method is easy provided your tool offers the facility. It also has the advantage that there is no confusion about whether a line of code is commented out or not, and it avoids any difficulty with nested comments and similar issues.

2. Your language may have a second comment syntax, specifically for multi-line comments. This means that there is some special combination of characters that marks the beginning of a comment, and a different special combination that marks the end of a comment. Everything that follows the begin-comment

sequence is ignored, until the end-comment sequence is found. In Java, C, etc., the beginning and end sequences are /* and */; in Haskell, {- and -}. Python does not have a true multi-line comment syntax. The advantage of this method is that it gives an easy way to comment out large blocks of code even in a dumb editor. However, there can be issues when you comment out a block of code that itself includes comments, and it may not be visually obvious which lines are commented out.

My preference is generally for the first of these two ways of commenting out chunks of code. It is – surprisingly, perhaps – a topic on which heated arguments between experts can occur, however. Recall the advice to find a body of reputable code in your language: you might like to see what is done there, and follow suit.

Once you know how to comment out code, should you do that, or should you delete it?

The advantage of commenting code out is that if in a few minutes you realise you do want it after all, it's a simple matter to uncomment it; and if you need something similar, it can be a good memory jogger.

The advantage of deleting it is that it keeps your code looking clean and simple: you have a better chance of being able to see all the important active code at once, which makes it easier to think straight.

How to decide? I recommend asking yourself *how sure you are* that you aren't going to want this code again. If you are pretty sure you won't, go ahead and delete it. If you think you very well may, comment it out for now, but remember to think about it again a bit later: don't let commented-out code sit around, getting in the way and distracting you, for weeks or longer. This is where a version control system is reassuring – if you have a version checked in containing that code (maybe commented out, if the code didn't work), you can always get it back if you need it.

One thing you definitely shouldn't do is leave code looking as though it is in use, when it is not.

Terminology: Dead or unreachable code

A section of your program code is *unreachable* if it can never be executed. For example, if you write a function as part of your program, but your program never calls it (nor makes it available for a client program to call) then that function is unreachable. You may hear *dead code* used as a synonym for unreachable code. Some sources use it, instead, to refer to code that *is* executed, but does not contribute to the intended behaviour of the program. For example, if your program calls a function, but never uses the result of the function call, then the function may be considered dead, but not unreachable.

Tidy up as you go. For example, if you write a function and then don't call it from anywhere, get rid of that code, at least by commenting it out, unless you know *for sure* that it will be used shortly. You might be tempted to think that it's doing no harm to leave the code there; after all, if it isn't called, any bug in it isn't exercised, so does it matter? However, unused code gets in your way and can be confusing. For example, when you search for a bug, you may waste time looking at that code, even though it can't possibly be the cause of the bug. Even if you are using an IDE which makes clear, e.g. using a colour change, that some code is unreachable, it still gets in the way by taking up screen space that could be better used. Get rid of it. As the agile programming people say, YAGNI.[1]

---

1 You Ain't Gonna Need It.

> **Tip**
>
> If you find yourself reluctant to delete a chunk of code that is not useful to you right now because you think you *are* going to need it – for example, it solves a problem you expect to have again, and you had to look up something tricky to get it right – then by all means do save it. Just don't save it inside a program where it is useless. I sometimes make a subfolder called CuttingRoomFloor for possibly useful snippets.

6.6 Backups and the Cloud

Making copies of your files, or using a version control system, can be an effective way to guard against losing your program because of your own accidental deletions. But what if the copies of the files, or the central repository of your version control system, are all stored on the same computer that you are working on, and then this computer dies, or is lost or stolen? In order to recover your work, you need it to be *backed up* in some way: that is, there needs to be a copy of the important files on some other computer, or on some external medium. If you are using a computer that is provided by your university or college, it is likely – but not certain! – that your files are automatically being backed up for you, and that there are computing support staff who can restore them for you if disaster strikes. If you are using your own equipment, you need to make your own arrangements to reduce the risk that you lose important work. As with version control, there is a range of approaches, from the fully manual – e.g. you get into the habit of copying your files onto a USB stick that you keep on a keyring, every time you finish a work session – to the fully automated. You could search

 automatic backup *your_operating_system*

for options. Today many people rely on storing their files *in the cloud* in some way – that is, on someone else's computer that you access via the internet. Google, Microsoft, Dropbox and others offer basic free services: you can keep your programs in a directory that gets automatically copied to their servers, and then, by logging into your account with the service, you can access them from anywhere on the internet. This can be very convenient day to day, especially if you regularly use several different computers and want to be able to work on your code on any one of them, as well as saving you in the case of disaster.

> **Tip**
>
> Backup plans that rely on you remembering to do something, such as copy your files or run the backup service, are useless if you do not remember. If you choose a plan that is not fully automatic, think about how you can turn the necessary actions into a habit that *feels* automatic, perhaps by connecting the new action with something you already do regularly.

A version control system lets you easily get back any earlier version you checked in; a cloud service lets you easily get back the current version from any computer. What if you want to combine these advantages? The obvious idea is to keep your version control repository in the cloud – but, especially if more than one person is using the repository, this can be dangerous because the services are not designed for this use, and corruption of the repository can result. A better idea is to use GitHub or another dedicated cloud-based version control system. Their *raison d'être* is to let teams of people collaborate from anywhere in the world, but you can use them for single-person projects such as coursework too.

However, one word of warning: if you decide to use a system, such as GitHub, that has the potential to make your files available to other people, you must think carefully about who should have access to what. For example, if you are working on an assessed exercise, you will normally not be allowed to give anyone else access to your solution – that would facilitate cheating, and is often penalised just as heavily as using someone else's solution. Examiners usually take the view that it is your responsibility to understand who has access to your files, so make sure you do!

Some people like to build up a publicly accessible repository of their code, which they can point at in job applications, etc. That's an idea, but it can backfire if you end up with old code still around after you've learned to write better – and once you put something on the internet, you can't guarantee it ever goes away! Consider more cautious alternatives, such as sending samples of your code direct to people you'd like to see them.

Tip

Be cautious about letting people you don't know see your code.

7

How to Test Your Program

You've written enough of your program that it's possible to run it; how do you find out whether it's right, so that you can fix it if it isn't? Well, you run it, and see if it does what you expect. For a really simple program, that may be all there is to say.

> **Python example**
>
> ```python
> print("Hello,_World!")
> ```

We run the program, observe that it prints "Hello, World!", and conclude that it is correct.

What did we do there, though? We implicitly understood

- that the program did not need to be given any command-line arguments, or any other specific context, in order to operate;
- that what it was supposed to do was to print "Hello, World!" to the usual place where we expect to see program output (known as *standard out*).

> **Terminology: Specification**
>
> A *specification* for a program is a description of what it is supposed to do. It may be very detailed, saying exactly what the program should do under any circumstances; or it may be *loose*, giving only a small part of the information the programmer will need.

Of course most programs are more complicated than this. They take input or operate in a context of some kind, and what they do may depend on that context. It may not be trivial to understand exactly what the program should do in a particular case. This is where tests come in. When you write a test down, you create a record of something you understand about the program's intended behaviour. This saves you effort: re-reading the test should be easier than going through the understanding process again. If you repeatedly run the same tests on the program as you develop it, you can satisfy yourself that you are improving the program, and if you accidentally change it in such a way that it behaves wrongly in a context where earlier it behaved correctly, you can fix it immediately. (See Chapter 9 – fixing a bug immediately after you introduce it is much easier than fixing it later!)

Terminology: Test

A *test* for a program is a specific context in which to run the program, including any necessary data, together with a specification of what the program should do in that context.

7.1 Manual Testing

Provided you know how to run your program, including how to set up its context – for example, give it any arguments it needs – and you know how to observe what your program does, you can do systematic testing. You do not need any special tools; a text file or a piece of paper will do. Just write down a list of tests: describe the context, and the required results. For example, suppose you have written a program slightly more sophisticated than Hello World, called `greeter`, that is supposed to take an argument and print out "Hello" followed by that argument. You might write:

List of tests

1. `greeter Rahul` outputs `Hello Rahul`
2. `greeter sue` outputs `Hello sue`
3. `greeter Jane Smith` outputs `Hello Jane`
4. ...

Now, systematically testing your program consists of going down the list and running your program once for each test, giving the appropriate context and checking for correct results.

As you write the tests, you will probably find yourself mentally formulating a concise description of what the program does. The third test in the panel shows that our initial description of the program was not fully detailed: assuming we got that test correct, when we give the `greeter` program the argument `Jane Smith` it is supposed to print `Hello Jane`, not `Hello Jane Smith`. This is the kind of detail you will need to be very careful about. After clarifying that, we might have a more precise specification, such as "the program outputs "Hello" followed by the first word of the input, exactly as given". A precise specification may be really useful if you have to change the program in future. Once you've gone to the trouble of getting it clear in your head, consider putting it into your program as a comment. In this case, the comment has the effect of telling anyone reading your code that it is deliberate that it only prints the first word of the argument.

Tip

Any time you do write down your program's specification, be sure to keep it up to date, if the intended behaviour of the program changes later!

Even if your program is capable of taking several inputs without restarting, for example using a loop, do start your program afresh for each test. Otherwise there may be some state that is set up by one test and then used in another. If you want to test how your program behaves when it's given several inputs in one run, that's a separate test.

7.2 Basic Automated Testing

Running your program by hand for each test, and comparing the results with what you expect by eye each time, gets tedious very fast. The next step is to get the computer to do some of the tedious bits.

There are different ways to do this, and you won't want to go far along this route before moving to using a proper testing framework (which we will discuss in Section 7.3 below), otherwise, you'll find yourself writing your own testing framework. Still, it can be a good way to get started.

The first thing you need is an automatic way to run exactly the code you want to test. That's easiest if it's simply a function. Then what a test has to do is to call your function, with some arguments if appropriate, compare what the function returns with what it should return, and complain if the two are different. Here is a classic way to do that in Python. The function we are testing is called `greeter`. Its source is not shown below, but it takes one string argument. Each test is just a function. `test_greeter_one_word` invokes the `greeter` function with the argument "Jane", and *asserts* that the result should be "Hello Jane". Many languages have a built-in assert statement (or function) that works like this: it can be very useful. Python's takes an extra argument which is a string to be printed if the test fails.

Python example

```python
def test_greeter_one_word():
    assert greeter("Jane") == "Hello Jane",\
            "Should be Hello Jane"

def test_greeter_two_words():
    assert greeter("Jane Smith") == "Hello Jane",\
            "Should be Hello Jane"

if __name__ == "__main__":
    test_greeter_one_word()
    test_greeter_two_words()
    print("Tests passed")
```

Things get only slightly more complicated when you want to test functions which are methods of a class. Let us look at the use of a "testing main" in Java. Your first few programs in Java may well have all their code inside a main method, like this:

Java example

```java
public class HelloWorld {
  public static void main(String[] args) {
    System.out.println("Hello, World!");
  }
}
```

If, however, you've gone to the next stage and written a class with some actual behaviour – e.g. some *instance methods* – you can use the main method to create an instance of the class and try out the methods. For example:

```java
public class SomeClass {
  // constructor and various methods...
  public static void main(String[] args) {
    SomeClass objectToTest = new SomeClass();
    int result1 = objectToTest.firstMethod();
    if (result1 != 42) {
      // print that something went wrong
    }
    // and so on
  }
}
```

If you wrote several classes, you can even give each of them its own testing main.

The testing main was useful for testing methods within your program, but it did not let you see the behaviour of your program as a whole – if you're using the main method for testing, you're not using it for its intended purpose of starting the whole program running. We might say, a testing main is more useful for *unit testing* than for *system testing*.

Terminology: Unit test

A *unit test* tests some particular unit of a program – e.g. a class – using a well-defined interface to that unit. It checks that that unit, considered in isolation from the rest of the program, meets its specification.

Terminology: System test

A *system test* tests a whole system, using the same interface that the system's users will eventually use. It checks that the system as a whole meets its specification.

To do system testing, we need to run the whole program from the outside – invoke it as a user would, give it input as a user would, and see whether the outputs and behaviour are what we expect. For simple programs you can often do that by using another program to start yours, capturing the output, and comparing the results. Scripting languages with good string handling facilities, like Python or Perl, are good language choices for the testing program. Just for fun, here's an example of using a small program in Perl to test a small program that's written in Python.

Perl example

```
$argument = 'Jane';
$expected = 'Hello␣Jane';
chomp ($result = `python greeter.py $argument`);
($result eq $expected)
    or die "Got␣$result,␣expected␣$expected";
print "Test␣passed";
```

Here the expression in backticks `...` invokes the Python program, with the argument we're testing it on, exactly as we'd do manually on the command line, and the result is saved in the variable `$result`. (The `chomp` just removes the newline that finishes the program's output, saving us from having to include that in every `expected`.) Then we compare the actual result with the expected result, and complain if the two are different. We show just one test

here, but of course, we could use a function to do the same thing
on many different pairs of argument and expected result. We can
use a program like this to test any other program, written in any
language: we just have to invoke it in the test program as we would
on the command line. Perl happens to be a convenient language
to write such a test program in, but my main reason for using Perl
here was to emphasise that the testing program does not have to be
in the same language as the program you are testing. You can do it
in your favourite language as well: have a go.

A word of warning, though: once you start developing your
own code to test your program, it can be easy to let it get over-
complicated. Somehow keeping test code clean and understandable
doesn't feel as important as keeping the code it's testing clean
and understandable ... but really, it should do, because you will
spend at least as much time using and modifying your test code as
any other code. Once you understand what you need, it is worth
investing in learning how to do proper automated testing using a
reliable, reusable testing framework provided by someone else.

7.3 Proper Automated Testing

Once upon a time, in fact until the late 1990s, programmers rou-
tinely used to develop their own code for managing unit tests. In
large organisations like the one I worked for in the early 1990s,
there was often some kind of testing framework – code for managing and running tests – maintained "in house", just at and for that
organisation. That meant at least that we didn't have to develop
the same code to do that stuff again, every time we started a new
project. Perhaps there were other testing frameworks available, but
none of them were famous, and as a young software developer I
didn't come across them.

Then came JUnit, the first popular unit testing framework. JUnit
supports unit testing for Java; since what it does is really not rocket
science, and it proved useful, there are now versions for many

popular programming languages (and some unpopular ones). Try searching

 unit testing *your_language*

and see what comes up; if there's a thing called somethingUnit described as being for your language, it'll probably be similar to JUnit for Java. (You could also look at the JUnit Wikipedia page.) JUnit makes it easy to write unit tests for Java programs, and then provides a framework for running the tests, which is incorporated into most IDEs. You'll typically get a simple graphical interface showing a green bar if all your tests pass, and a red bar if some don't, together with a way to get to the test that failed and the code it failed on. Going into detail here is beyond the scope of this book, but there are some good JUnit tutorials[1] and it's well worth learning. Unfortunately, while using JUnit is simple, really understanding how the JUnit framework itself works requires a more in-depth knowledge of Java than you'll get in an introductory course, so you may have to take some things on trust.

Terminology: Framework

Like a library, a framework provides functionality designed to be used in many other programs. The difference is that using a framework exerts more control over the structure of your program than using a library does. Rather than calling library functions when you choose, you write functions (e.g. tests, in the case of JUnit) that the framework code will call. This is the Hollywood Principle: "don't call us, we'll call you".

---

1 One I like is www.vogella.com/tutorials/JUnit/article.html, or for a gentler introduction, you might try www.tutorialspoint.com/junit/.

7.4 What Tests Should You Have?

- If the task description included some examples to explain what was wanted, you should definitely include those examples in your test set.
- Include the simplest possible inputs to your program. If your program takes an integer, what should it return if you give it 0? 1? −1? If it takes a string, what should it do with the empty string? With a single-character string?
- Are any values obviously risky, i.e. do they feel like inputs likely to expose a problem? These are often those that are at or close to values that are special in the task description, or in your solution. For example, if your function takes x as input and has an `if` statement that is supposed to do something different depending on whether x is less than 100 or greater, make sure you test with 99, 100 and 101.
- Think about the classes of inputs: are they all represented? For example, if oddness and evenness matters in your program, do you have a test of an odd number and an even number?
- Think about the classes of expected behaviour: are they all represented? For example, if your program should return a boolean, do you have tests that should return false, as well as tests that should return true? (This is curiously easy to forget: it's a kind of *positive bias*.)
- Whenever you discover a bug in your program, make sure you keep a test that would have caught that bug, i.e. that the buggy program fails but the fixed program passes. This makes sure you never re-introduce the bug. Running such tests is called *regression testing*: a *regression* is when something goes wrong that used to work properly.
- Test things that should not happen: for example, does your program react as well as you want it to, if the user does something wrong, like giving input of the wrong type?

Paradoxically, a successful test is one that finds a bug – because any programmer sometimes introduces bugs, and the aim of testing is to detect them as soon as possible. When you write tests, you should be trying to get your program to misbehave. This can be quite hard – if you wrote the program, it's natural to want it to succeed and the subconscious temptation is to give it easy tests! If you're doing a course, you might like to imagine your mean instructor trying to take marks off you. If you find the bugs first, your instructor will not. Often, even in settings where it would not be allowed to show your code to another student, it will be allowed to show your tests to one another. Could you get together with some friends and pool your tests, making it a friendly competition to cause each other's programs to misbehave?

The Lauren bug

Margaret Hamilton, who worked on the Apollo space missions and led the team developing software for the first moon landing, has one of the earliest stories about how vital it can be to test what should not happen. She tells in an interview (Corbyn, 2019) how she once took her small daughter Lauren to work with her, and Lauren, pressing keys randomly, caused a mission simulation to crash by invoking a procedure at the wrong point. Hamilton was concerned that an astronaut might do the same thing for real, and thought the software should be changed to prevent it. Senior people at MIT and NASA said that real astronauts would never make such a mistake – until they did, at which point the software was changed!

7.5 When Should You Write Tests?

Some expert readers will complain that I should have introduced testing much earlier. The reason I chose not to is that in order to write tests you have to be able to program a bit; you have to start somewhere. Now that you have the skills to write tests, though, you should seriously consider adopting test-driven development and using it for the rest of your life.

Terminology: Test-driven development

Test-driven development (TDD) goes like this:

1. Write a test that you would like to pass, but fails.
2. Write just enough code to make all the tests pass.
3. Improve the code if possible, and check that the tests still pass.

You do this from the very beginning – so the very first code you write is a test – and repeat until the program is finished, i.e. it passes every test it should pass and cannot be improved.

By writing the test before you write the code that it is testing, you check that you understand exactly what the code should do. By writing just one test at a time, you keep your increments small, so that if you make a mistake it is easy to understand and fix. By rerunning all of the tests each time, you ensure that you don't break previously working code.

People who adopt TDD are often evangelical about it, and you will even hear it said that it is irresponsible to use any other approach. Still, many expert and professional developers do not use it. I think, in reality, that how well it works depends more on what code you are writing, and in what environment, than the evangelists sometimes acknowledge. Perhaps, too, part of the reason it isn't universal yet is that some people actively enjoy debugging their code. Using TDD makes you less likely to introduce challenging bugs into your code that you can then have the "pleasure" of removing!

7.6 Property-Based Testing

An approach that began in the world of Haskell but has been spreading, especially to other functional languages, is known as *random testing* or *property-based testing*. The original property-based testing tool is QuickCheck, for Haskell. The idea is that your function, or your whole program, is given *lots* of different random inputs, and the outputs are automatically checked using some kind of specification, which you give as a *property* that the function's input and output should satisfy. If your program has a bug that means the property can fail on some input, there's a decent chance that when the random tester throws, say, 10,000 inputs at your program, at least one of them will demonstrate the bug. The clever part comes next: the testing tool then goes through a simplification process aimed at finding the simplest way to cause that buggy behaviour, and that's what it shows you, for you to debug.

The property you test might be very basic (very *loose* or impoverished), e.g. it might just capture that the program should not crash. Or it might be extremely sophisticated, laying out the relationship between the input and the output in detail. In practice, it is rare to test a perfectly detailed property, because the task of writing one tends to be as hard as, and closely related to, the task of writing the program. Generally, the property only captures some of the information about what the program should do, so if the property is true, it doesn't guarantee that the program is correct: there might still be a bug that this property cannot expose, no matter how many inputs are tested. However, if the property turns out to be *false*, it does show that there's a problem.

Here's an example. Suppose our function `factor` is supposed to take a positive integer and return a list of its prime factors (with multiplicity, so that, for example, `factor 18` might return `[2,3,3]`). We could test it like this:

Haskell example

```
import Test.QuickCheck
-- function factor omitted...
prop_factor :: Int -> Bool
prop_factor i = product (factor i) == i
```

The function `prop_factor` takes an integer, and returns true if, on that integer, the function `factor` returns a list which satisfies a basic reasonableness property: multiplying together the supposed prime factors does produce the original integer. If some test of this property fails, there is definitely a problem with the `factor` function. However, `prop_factor` does not catch all possible problems that the `factor` function could have. For example, it does not check that the elements of the list that `factor` returns are really prime numbers. Indeed, the `factor` function that simply returned the one-element list containing just its input would always pass. Nevertheless, such simple, partial testing properties can be easy to write and very useful for catching the kind of errors programmers typically make. Suppose someone misunderstands the specification, and instead of returning a list of the prime factors with multiplicity, their `factor` returns a list of the *distinct* prime factors, so that given 18 it returns `[2,3]`. When I wrote that buggy `factor` and used QuickCheck to check the property `prop_factor`, I saw:

```
*Main> quickCheck prop_factor
*** Failed! Falsifiable (after 7 tests):
4
*Main>
```

That is, QuickCheck had to run a total of seven tests, but it only showed me one example of an input that makes the test fail: 4, where the buggy `factor` will return `[2]`, instead of the correct answer, `[2,2]`. Given this really simple failing example, it is easy to see what went wrong.

Famous quotations about testing

- "A successful test is one that finds a bug."

  Anon.

  You need to put yourself into the frame of mind where you *want* your program to fail – otherwise, you risk only writing the tests that your program will pass, which is pointless.

- "Every bug found in testing is one the customer doesn't find."

  Anon.

  For people who have customers they care about, this idea can help motivate them to get into the right frame of mind. Of course, it's only really true if you go on to fix the bug, and keep it fixed … which is one reason for doing *systematic* testing. When you're a student, you may find it useful to think of the person who is going to mark your work as the customer.
- "Program testing can be used to show the presence of bugs, but never to show their absence!"

  Edsger Dijkstra (Djikstra, 1970)

  The philosophical point here is that if your program has infinitely many possible inputs, and you only run finitely many tests, then in principle, it might still fail on some input you haven't tested. To be sure that your program works on every input, you have to study the code of the program and prove that it is correct. There's a large field of study of software testing concerned with how to pick enough of the right tests to be sure that if certain kinds of bug existed in the program, we would find them. For a start, you'd like to have every line of your code, that could ever be run, run in the process of doing some test – otherwise, a line that was missed out might contain a bug.
- "Beware of bugs in the above code; I have only proved its correctness, not tried it."

  Don Knuth (Knuth, 1977)

  This tongue-in-cheek antidote to the Dijkstra quotation above reminds us that proof, like programming, is a human activity. Unfortunately, there can be bugs in your proof, just as there can be bugs in your program. Especially, it's easy to incorporate the same mistaken assumptions into both!

8

How to Make Your Program Clear

In discussing what a "good program" is (Chapter 2), we claimed it should be clearly written. It is natural that when you start to learn to program, you focus on making your program correct. You may find yourself resenting any suggestion that your correct program could still be improved: if it does what it is supposed to do, isn't that all that matters? In this chapter we explain why it is very much in your interest to write your code as clearly as possible, and discuss how to do so.

8.1 How Will Writing Clear Code Help You?

We said that a program is a set of instructions for a computer, and of course it is that – but even more importantly, the program is an explanation for a human reader of *what the computer is being instructed to do*. That reader might be you, as you initially write the code; someone trying to mark your code, or give you help with it; or someone (perhaps you, later) trying to improve it or extend it. The better your code communicates what the computer will do, the easier all of these tasks will be.

> **Tip**
>
> Always make your code as easy to read as you can. Even if you have to spend some time clarifying it, you will save time overall, as it becomes easier to keep your code correct.

At the beginning of their programming lives, people usually under-estimate the importance of this topic. There is a tendency to think that, since you are a beginner and not using advanced features of the language, any code that you can write will automatically be easy for an expert – or for you, on a later occasion – to read. However, when you write code, you may be holding in mind a lot of information, accumulated as you consider the problem and how to solve it. Someone reading the code later does not start with the same mental state. Moreover, the feeling that you understand what you have written can be misleading: striving to write your code as clearly as possible will minimise the risk that you have overlooked some mistake.

Consider a simple Java exercise: the setAgeRating method in a Film class. Any Film has an ageRating which has to be one of 12, 15 or 18. This setAgeRating method takes an integer argument. If the argument is one of 12, 15, 18, then this is to be saved as the new value of the Film's ageRating. Otherwise, the method is supposed to do nothing.

Here's an example[1] of how *not* to write this method:

Java example (don't do this!)

```
public void setAgeRating(int l){
        if(l==12){
                   this.ageRating= 12;}
else if(l == 15)
                   {this.ageRating =15;}
else{this.ageRating = 18;}
}
```

---

1 Adapted from real student code by *improving* it.

Here's a better (though arguably still imperfect) version.

Java example

```java
public void setAgeRating(int a) {
  if (a == 12 || a == 15 || a == 18) {
    this.ageRating = a;
  } // otherwise, do nothing at all.
}
```

Before you read on, compare the two versions. What problems can you see with the first?

8.2 Comments

We will start with the topic of comments, because it seems to be what people think of first, when you ask them what they can do to make their code clearer. In the example above, I chose to include a comment "otherwise, do nothing at all". Why? Because I found it slightly surprising that, if the argument to the function was not one of 12, 15, or 18, we were supposed to do nothing at all – not even output an error message. I included the comment to remind myself, and any future reader, that this surprising behaviour was deliberate, not a sign that the code was unfinished or wrong. This is an informal way to handle such a situation; in a professional situation, you might be writing a full specification of the method, perhaps even with references out to an agreed requirements document. If you were using test-driven development, you would, of course, have a test that gave an argument other than 12, 15 or 18 and checked that ageRating did not change.

I'm going to give one piece of advice that may feel a bit odd, and may even seem to contradict things you've been told, but which is born of many years of experience:

> **Tip**
>
> Don't write too many comments, especially early on.

The reason is two-fold. The most important is that people often write comments to explain lines of code that are unclear to them. If the code is unclear because it isn't written in the best possible way, it's much better to rewrite the code, paying attention to the other issues discussed in this chapter, rather than adding a comment. The best way to write code is: so lucidly that it does not need comments.

A secondary issue is that sometimes people write fully documented code while their understanding of it is still changing fast. This is to some extent a matter of personal choice: if you find this helps *you* to think straight, go ahead. But if you're writing comments that are aimed at someone else (a future maintainer, or someone marking your code) then it's often more efficient to write comments when your code is approaching steady state. Comments that are out of date can be positively harmful.

> **Tip**
>
> "If the code and the comments disagree, both are probably wrong."
>
> *Norm Schryer* (attributed, Bentley, 1988)
>
> Bear this in mind when you read other people's code, but especially when you write your own!

A question which you will encounter early on is: what should you assume about the readers of your code? Should you assume that they are experts in the programming language, for example? There's no substitute for thinking about who really will be reading the code.

If you are programming while taking a programming course, you, yourself, are probably the most important reader.

An implication of this is that it's OK to write comments that someone who was much more expert in the language than you are would not need. People often sneer at comments that explain how a programming language feature is being used, on the grounds that you should be able to assume the reader is competent. Indeed it's easy to go too far, and end up with code like:

Java example (don't do this!)

```
i++; // add 1 to i
```

That really is excessive. However, I have found that when I learn a new programming language, it's often helpful to add a comment the first time I use a tricky new language feature or library function. If I avoid doing so, too often I end up forgetting about it and having to look it up again in order to understand my own code. I tend to see such comments as temporary, and for my eyes only, and I take pleasure in deleting such comments later, once I'm confident I have internalised the point in question.

This brings us to the observation that there are different kinds of comments which serve different purposes. You may find it helpful to distinguish them in your mind. We just discussed comments whose purpose is to support someone new to the language or software environment. Other kinds of comments include:

• Documentation of chunks of code. For example, you might write a comment above a function definition to explain what the function does, or close to a calculation to explain why this is the right calculation to do.

- More specifically, a contract that a chunk of code is guaranteed to obey.

Terminology: Contract

A *contract* for a piece of code is a precise expression of something about how the code is supposed to behave. A function or method may be given a *pre-condition* and/or a *post-condition*. The pre-condition says what the code is allowed to assume is true before it is executed; this must, therefore, be ensured by any caller of the code. The post-condition says what the code will ensure is true after it has been executed (provided its pre-condition was satisfied). A part of the program that contains some data – such as a class, or a loop – may be given an *invariant*, which says something must be true "always" (strictly speaking: at certain important points, such as the start of the loop, or when a method of an object of the class is called).

For example, if you are writing a function that takes an integer argument i, but you have decided (perhaps because it is part of the specification of an exercise you are doing) that the function will only handle positive integers, you might write

```
Precondition: i > 0
```

as a comment to warn readers about the assumption.

- Design notes. For example, if you tried coding something the obvious way, found that was too slow, and found a less obvious way that was better, you might include a comment to explain that.
- Notes to self. For example, if you have an idea about how you might want to improve the program in future, but you don't want to make the improvement right now, you might write a comment to remind yourself.

8.3 Names

> **Tip**
>
> Names are absolutely crucial. Good choice of names will help you, and everyone else, to read the code, and hence reduce the number of comments that you need to write.

Let us start with the part that is easiest to get right: use the conventions that are standard in your language, when you decide how to capitalise your names and how to handle names that consist of several words joined together. Having a fixed set of conventions that you always follow makes you – and anyone else who has to edit your program – much less likely to mistype a name, e.g. writing `do_something` when it should have been `doSomething`. It makes it possible to remember a name by how it sounds; you don't have to remember how the words are put together, if by convention that is always done the same way. Therefore, pay attention to what these conventions are. For example, Java's conventions include the following.

- Classes begin with a capital letter, e.g. `Customer`.
- Attribute names are lower case, e.g. `name`.
- Method names are in what is called *camel case*[2] e.g. `doSomething`.
- Classes and attributes are named with nouns or noun phrases. Class names are almost[3] always singular (`Customer`, not `Customers`): the name describes an object of the class, not the collection of all objects of the class.

---

2 Think about the humps! In Python, appropriately, we write method names in *snake case*, e.g. `do_something`, instead.
3 The exception is when a single object is best described by a plural noun. E.g. a single object of class `Preferences` might describe all of one user's preferences.

• Methods are named with verbs, or verb phrases, e.g. `doSomething`, `getName`, `setName`.

Towards the end of this list we are starting to get to less trivial matters: how do you choose a name so that it conveys information optimally to the reader? A reasonable question to ask yourself is: is there a name that would tell the reader more of what they need to know? Do not duplicate type information: avoid calling a string variable `theString`, for example. If you're working in a language where types are explicit in the program text, such a name is entirely redundant; and even if you are not, you can probably do better. Think about what the thing you are naming is representing. If you were explaining the code to someone, what would you say about this thing? Can the words you would say become its name?

It is better to use a whole word as a name than an abbreviation, unless you are sure that the abbreviation is so standard that everyone reading the program will know what it means and expect it to be used. This is especially important if there are many related names in your program.

For example, suppose "customer" occurs as part of the name of many things in your program, and is sometimes, but not always, abbreviated to `cust`. Then inevitably, a programmer working with the code will sometimes guess wrongly whether or not to abbreviate it this time. It would be even worse if "customer" were abbreviated to `cst` in a context where "cost" was also sometimes involved!

In order to resist the temptation to abbreviate, learn good ways to avoid typing long names too often. An IDE, or a sophisticated editor with its autocompletion feature (see Chapter 5), can help here. For example, in Eclipse, Ctrl-Space will (usually!) attempt to complete the thing you started typing. In Emacs, Meta-/ will do the same, rather less intelligently.

At the same time as avoiding confusing abbreviations, you need to stop your lines of code getting unmanageably long, like this:

Java example (don't do this!)

```
verySpecialCustomer.lookupHomeOrHomeBusinessAddress(preferredCustomerId,monthOfTheYear)
```

How do you reconcile these conflicting forces? You could solve the physical problem of the line being too long by splitting it: see the panel at the end of this chapter for more on that. However, that would not solve the real problem: the reason why this line is too long is that the names are too complex. The key is to choose exactly the right names, and to structure your program in such a way that everything *has* a name that feels right without being too long. That thought takes us beyond local considerations towards overall software design; we will have a little more to say about this in Chapter 10.

The further away from its definition the name might have to be interpreted, the more important it is that it be informative. Suppose you write a function that, because of the rules of the programming language, can only be called from inside a particular section of your code. (An example would be a private method in Java, or a function defined in a where clause in Haskell.) You already know that someone thinking about calling this function is looking at this section of your code, so it is fine if the name only makes sense to someone who is doing that. On the other hand, if your function can be used from anywhere in the program, it had better have a generally understandable name.

In particular, it's OK to use single letters for the names of variables that are only used within a short section of code. I did this in the example that opened this chapter, where I chose to use a as the name of the argument to my setAgeRating method. I could have used a meaningful name such as newAgeRating, and some people would consider that better; it's arguable. One thing that is not controversial, though, is that the use of letter l as an argument name in the "bad" example is awful, because

it is too easily confused with digit 1; similarly, avoid O and o.
Adopt any standard conventions that exist in your language about
which single letters to use in what contexts. Typically, i, j, k, n are
integers, especially loop variables and/or indexes into arrays. s is
often a string. If you are programming with the head and tail of a
list, the name for the tail is often the plural form of the name of
the head, e.g. (x:xs).

> **Tip**
>
> It is normal to realise, part of the way through writing a
> program, that there is a better name than the one you first
> chose. Welcome this: it's a sign that you are improving your
> understanding of the problem and the program that solves it.

Learn good ways to change the name of a variable, for when you
realise the name isn't very good. Again, an IDE can make your
life much easier. In Eclipse, the Refactor menu includes a Rename
option that works quite intelligently. In an editor, the find-and-
replace feature is often convenient enough, especially if the name
you're trying to change isn't too short.

8.4 Layout and Whitespace

Use a standard, consistent layout for your program. This is one
place where using an IDE (see Chapter 5) really helps. In Eclipse,
use the Format option on the Source menu for this. If you want
or need to, you can change many aspects of how that will fix the
formatting of your code, in the settings.

However, an advantage of having your layout fixed automatically is that it can relieve you of the burden of deciding how much
you care: it can give you layout which is consistent enough to satisfy
the most pedantic of colleagues, even if you yourself are inclined
to be more flexible. Here's a classic example. In languages that use
curly brackets to surround blocks of code, there is a question about
their placement. Some programmers would write

Java example

```java
public String getName() {
  return name;
}
```

while others prefer

Java example

```java
public String getName()
{
  return name;
}
```

The computer does not care. Few readers really care. *But* if a single program ends up with an inconsistent mixture of these two styles, it becomes subtly harder to read, and to edit correctly. When you are a student, the best advice is not to mess with the settings.

Similarly, you will find there are conventions about where to put spaces within lines of code: compare, among many other possibilities:

Java example (don't do this!)

```java
  int i = f(7);
  int i=f(7);
  int i = f( 7);
  int i=f( 7 ) ;
```

Again, the point is not that any of these is objectively better than any other, though you will sometimes find people who will argue it. The point is that people will find the code more readable if it uses one convention, consistently. (The first line in the example above is normal in Java.)

Here is a version of the opening example in which I have swapped the terrible name l for a and fixed the layout, but changed nothing else:

Java example

```java
public void setAgeRating(int a) {
  if (a == 12) {
    this.ageRating = 12;
  } else if (a == 15) {
    this.ageRating = 15;
  } else {
    this.ageRating = 18;
  }
}
```

Have you spotted the correctness problem yet?

Different languages have different conventions, which may be more or less uniformly followed. Unlike many languages, Python has a single, widely followed style guide, PEP 8, written by the developers of the language. Carefully written, with many examples, it tells you everything you might want to know about how to format and lay out Python code. If your language has such a style guide, use it! Otherwise, as we advised in Chapter 4, pick a body of reputable code in your language to use as a comparator.

Tip

Remember that it's possible that code written by your instructors is not setting a good example! If they teach several languages, with conflicting conventions, their fingers may be confused.

Tabs and spaces

A common source of confusion, which can be a root cause of layout problems, is confusion concerning how and when to use tab characters and space characters as whitespace in program text.

Usually, you get a space character when you hit the space bar on your keyboard, and you get a tab character when you hit the tab key (which is usually on the far left of the keyboard, looking something like ⎡ → ⎤. If you are not familiar with both, have a play in a plain text file. You will probably find that the visual effect of starting a line with a tab character is similar to that of starting it with some number of space characters, usually 2 or 4. (A tab character in the middle of a line has more interesting behaviour.) However, what is placed in the text file is different. A tab is a single character, which just happens to be displayed like a number of space characters.

The problems begin when you mix tabs and spaces. Let us suppose that you are working in an editor with "tab width" 4 – that is, where one tab character at the beginning of a line is displayed the same way as four space characters. Now, if you write one line beginning with a tab character, and the next line beginning with four space characters, they will line up neatly. If, however, you then open the same file in an editor with tab width 2, the lines will no longer start in the same position.

In an attempt to be helpful, IDEs and programming modes in editors may intercept your keystrokes and do something different from what you expect. For example, in Python, whitespace is significant, and spaces are preferred to tabs (e.g. PEP 8 tells you to use spaces). For this reason, the Python mode in Emacs will insert four space characters, not one tab character, when you type the tab key. Similarly, Haskell is sensitive to how code is indented, and a good rule of thumb is to make sure that your Haskell files contain space characters, not tab characters. By contrast, the meaning of a Java program does not depend at all on the whitespace in it, and Java programmers quite commonly use tabs.

If you get strange layout behaviour when you look at the same file in two different ways, it is worth suspecting that there may be tab characters in the file which are being rendered as different numbers of spaces. How you test and fix this depends on exactly what tools you are using: Atom, for example, has a Show Invisibles setting which helpfully makes the difference between tabs and spaces visible.

Amusingly, a 2017 survey[a] found that "coders who use spaces for indentation make more money than ones who use tabs, even if they have the same amount of experience".

As a general rule, I recommend you use spaces rather than tabs: given that today's tools can insert the right number of spaces automatically, tab characters are more trouble than they are worth. Before you get into the habit of touching the tab key, check that what it inserts into the file is space characters. If not, either change your editor or IDE configuration so that it does insert spaces, or don't use it. A search such as

 your_editor_or_IDE tabs spaces

will probably lead you to instructions on how to set up your editor or IDE.

---

a https://stackoverflow.blog/2017/06/15/developers-use-spaces-make-money-use-tabs/

8.5 Structure and Idiom

So far we have talked only about small, local aspects of code clarity: things you improve by changing individual lines or names. Of course bigger aspects of how you solve problems affect how easy your code is to read, too. This relates to *design* and we will only scratch the surface here.

Programming languages are used by communities of people, who collectively develop standard ways of doing things. If you do what the rest of the community does, you will be writing *idiomatic* code in your language, which will make your code easier for people in the community to understand quickly. You will also be taking advantage of accumulated experience in the language.

Terminology: Idiom

An *idiom* in a given programming language is a way to solve a common small problem that is normally used by people in the language community.

For example, there are many ways to write code that swaps the values of variables a and b. In Python, the idiomatic way to do this is:

Python example

```
a, b = b, a
```

This short, simple solution takes advantage of the way the Python language is defined (specifically, its defined order of evaluation).

Watch out for idioms in your language, by spotting fragments of code that appear repeatedly in code written by experienced people. It is a good exercise to identify the problem being solved and think about how else it could be solved, and about how you would solve it in any other languages you may know. Can you articulate why the idiomatic solution has become the preferred way?

What about how you organise the code at larger scales? Early in a programming course, you are likely to be told how to do that organisation, in each case. Once *you* are making decisions about what modules or classes to write, which pieces of functionality to place where, and how to manage the flow of control and of data in your program, clarity is a major concern. In our opening example, the "bad" version uses a sequence of `if` statements that the reader must follow through, while the "better" version uses just one, with a more complex condition. It takes advantage of the fact that the required behaviour, if the argument is one of 12, 15, 18, is the same in each case: set `ageRating` to that argument. Even without the comment, the simpler structure makes the overall behaviour clearer, and helps avoid bugs.[4]

Think about what a reader, trying to understand some aspect of your program, will need to understand, and try to place the relevant pieces of code close together. Avoid writing spaghetti code.

Terminology: Spaghetti code

Imagine printing out your program and drawing lines on the printout to represent the flow of control; for example, if one function calls another, you draw a line from the call to the definition of the function being called. If the resulting collection of lines is complicated and tangled, you have *spaghetti code*. It's likely to happen if, for example, two modules or classes each depend on the other in multiple ways.

The origin of the term is unclear. My father, W.G.R. Stevens, recalls using it when he was a programmer in the 1960s, and having to explain to a colleague[a] that he was not referring to short lengths of spaghetti tinned in tomato sauce, which were the commonest form of spaghetti in England at that time, but rather, to proper long spaghetti that you would get in a packet, or in an Italian restaurant!

---

a C.B.B. Grindley, who later wrote about it in a paper I have sadly been unable to trace

---

4 If you have not yet spotted the bug in the "bad" version, now is the time to ask yourself: what happens if we give argument 7 to the method? And what was supposed to happen?

This advice about high-level structuring may seem unsatisfactory because it is hard to decide which structure is best without considerable experience; you will inevitably learn partly from your mistakes. It turns out that a common concrete sign of possible problems with your current structure is that your lines of code get too long.

How long should a line of code be?

If you find yourself resizing a window, or scrolling horizontally, in order to see the whole of a line of your code, it is probably too long to comprehend efficiently. Even if you succeed in adjusting your own environment so that you can see the whole line, you may well be causing difficulty for someone else who has to read your code in future. Projects, and sometimes whole language communities, develop conventions about the maximum length of a line: for example, Python's PEP 8 prescribes that no line should be longer than 79 characters.

One way to tackle long lines is to split them. If you do this, consult your body of reputable code in your language to see what the conventions are about where a line may be split. Usually, though, a too-long line of code is a sign of an underlying problem, and it is better to fix that. Ask yourself:

* Is a name too long? If so, do not just abbreviate it: think about whether there is a better, shorter name. If not, perhaps the thing named should be split up?
* Has your logical structure become too deeply nested (e.g. do you have an `if` inside an `if` inside an `if`) so that the line starts with a lot of whitespace? If so, do not just reduce your indentation width: think about how you could improve the structure. Perhaps there is a chunk of nested code that should be a separate function?
* Do you have a complex expression involving several operators, functions or messages? These are often hard to understand however they are laid out; consider constructing your result in stages, naming the intermediate results carefully.

We will come back in Chapter 10 to discuss *how* you can improve the structure of your program when you need to, and Chapter 15 discusses resources beyond the scope of this book.

Still, much of the advice in this chapter is easy to follow from the beginning. If you get into the habit of choosing informative names, laying out your code clearly, and making good use of comments, you will save yourself time and stress.

9

How to Debug Your Program

So your program has a bug.

Terminology: Bug

A bug in a program is something wrong with it: usually a small, specific thing which you might whimsically picture as an insect curled up on a line of your code, even if you don't yet know which line or which insect. The term "bug" for a small error or glitch pre-dates computers, but the computing pioneer Grace Hopper famously used to tell a story about an actual moth recovered from an early electromechanical computer (the Harvard Mark II) where it was interfering with the operation of a program.

More formally, we sometimes talk about faults, errors and failures, with each term meaning something subtly different. You might find it interesting to look that up. "Bugs" will do for now, however.

First things first: how do you *know* your program has a bug? It might be that your compiler, interpreter or IDE is telling you there is a problem, before you even get to run your program. Or it might be that when you run the program, it does not behave correctly: perhaps a test fails, the program crashes, or you do not see what you expect to see.

Debugging has four steps to go through – and then a bonus fifth step, which is crucial to turning yourself into a *good* programmer.

1. *Recognising* that there is a bug at all. Congratulations, you've done that one. It may not feel like much of an achievement, but it is. If you had, for example, not bothered to compile your program, or not run your program on that input, perhaps you wouldn't have achieved it.
2. *Localising* the bug. That is, working out where in your program there is a problem.
3. *Understanding* the bug. That is, working out exactly what the problem is.
4. *Removing* the bug. That is, changing the program so that, at least in this one respect, it is correct (and will stay correct, because you have a suitable test to prevent regression).
5. The bonus step: as far as possible, ensuring that there are no other similar bugs in your program, and even better, that you never introduce a similar bug into any program you work on in future.

Localising and understanding the bug often go together: you may start out with a rough idea of where the bug is, but you may only get to understand precisely where it is once you understand exactly what's wrong. We'll talk about some routine techniques here: if they aren't enough and you need help, you may also want to look at Chapter 11, especially concerning how to build a *minimal non-working example*.

Tip

As you try to localise and understand a bug, *use all the information available*. Too often, students observe that something doesn't work – there is a compile-time or run-time error, or a failed test – but they do not pay close attention to the specific error message, or check which test fails and how. The information may look intimidating, but don't be put off. You will quickly learn to interpret it if you try every time.

Debugging situations divide into two classes, depending on whether you can run the program at all, or not.

9.1 **When You Can't Run Your Program Yet**

If your compiler, interpreter or IDE is telling you there is a problem which makes it impossible to run your program, then almost certainly it will also be making some attempt to help you to understand where and what the bug is, by giving you some kind of error message or marker.

Such error messages can (notoriously) be confusing, however. It is a difficult job to ensure that every error message clearly and correctly indicates what the problem is. It's even more difficult to design error messages that will be helpful even to a programmer who is only just getting started. So very likely it's not you – the error message really is hard to understand – but cut the tool developers some slack. If you read an error message and have no idea what it's trying to tell you, you will probably not be the first person with that problem. Try a search, copying and pasting the error message directly from where you see it into your search bar:

 your_language the_error_message

for example

 python TypeError: unsupported operand type(s)

Here are a few examples coming from a Java compiler.

Examples of Java error messages

```
error: '(' expected
error: reached end of file while parsing
error: cannot find symbol
error: unexpected type
```

Fortunately, the compiler gives, along with the basic error message, some further information – usually an indication of where in the file the error arose, but often other information as well, such as *what* symbol it was that the compiler couldn't find.

Tip

When an error message gives a line number, look at that line first – but bear in mind that the error may be earlier in your program, and only have been detected further on, at the given line number. For example, a missing semi-colon on one line may cause an error to be reported on the next line.

Terminology: Errors compared with warnings

Sometimes your compiler will give you a message involving the word "error", like those given above. Other times you may see messages involving the word "warning" instead. There is an important difference. An *error* is something you must fix before you go on – typically it has prevented your file from compiling at all. A *warning* is an indication that the compiler has detected something which is *probably* an indication that you've done something wrong. For example, compilers will often warn if they discover that your program contains unreachable code. You *can* ignore a warning, or even instruct the compiler not to give warnings – but it's usually a good idea not to. Some compilers are better than others at giving warnings that genuinely do indicate problems. If you get a kind of warning you haven't seen before, it's definitely worth spending a few minutes on investigating what's causing it and whether you can fix it. For example, in the case of unreachable code, you can delete it (or comment it out, if you think you might need it again in a moment).

Often there will be an obvious problem – a mistyped word or a missing bracket, for example – on or around the line number given in the error message. Sometimes, however, either the compiler will give no line number, or it will indicate a line that really looks perfectly fine to you. Now you benefit if you've been compiling as you go, or having your IDE do it for you. If you have a good idea of what has been changed or added since the last time there was no error, look suspiciously at those parts.

If you still don't see the problem, try commenting out code – replacing it with simpler code as necessary, e.g. replacing a complex calculation of an integer with constant 1 – until you do get a clean compilation, or, failing that, until you get a different error message.

Tip

Save a copy of your code before you do this, or make any other changes that you aren't sure will help, so that if an hour later you find a tiny change that fixes the problem, you don't have to do a lot of work undoing all the other changes you tried.

It can help to understand something about the activities that are undertaken in compiling your program text, starting from the text file that you typed, and ending up with an executable program. At this stage, a very rough idea will do. In particular, it is useful to understand whether an error arose during parsing, or whether your program parsed correctly but some problem turned up at a later stage.

Terminology: Parsing

Parsing of a program text is the process of building a structured representation of the program (an *abstract syntax tree*). This involves splitting the text up into chunks such as keywords, names and operators (*lexing*), and then checking that these chunks fit together in the way the language definition requires.

If you have an error message that tells you there was a problem parsing your program, you do not need to check more sophisticated issues like whether you are providing functions with arguments of the right types; your mistake will be something more basic, where your text somehow failed to match the patterns of the language definition. (This description is necessarily a bit vague, since we are not going into what parsing does in detail.)

It is common that several error messages arise from the same error: don't assume seven error messages means seven separate errors! Almost always, the first error message is the most useful one.

Story

Dmitri starts to do a Java exercise. Following the advice in Chapter 3 he writes only a few lines before he first compiles: just the outer wrapper of his class and its main function, without any functionality yet.

Java example (don't do this!)

```java
public class ExerciseOne {
  public static void main {String[] args) {
  }
}
```

He's surprised to find that when he compiles he already gets *three* error messages:

```
javac ExerciseOne.java
ExerciseOne.java:2: error: '(' expected
    public static void main {String[] args) {
                          ^
ExerciseOne.java:2: error: ';' expected
    public static void main {String[] args) {
                                          ^
ExerciseOne.java:4: error: reached end of file while parsing
}
 ^
3 errors
```

Fortunately, when he reads just the first error message, he finds it tells him rather clearly what the problem is: the compiler expected an opening round bracket, in line 2 of his file, and there's even a caret (^) to show exactly where in line 2. He sees that he had accidentally typed an opening curly bracket instead. He changes just this one character, saves the file, and tries the compilation again. All three error messages disappear, so he's in a good state to continue.

Type errors are a common kind of compile-time error – and the more powerful the language's type system is, i.e. the more problems it can rule out, the more common they are. If, as in Haskell, the type system is very sophisticated, the error messages are sometimes hard to interpret, because they may mention features of the type system that you have not yet met. We saw an example of this in the story in Chapter 3. Remember the option of searching for the error message online, if you get stuck. More often, though, the error message will tell you what the problem is in terms you can understand. Let us look at a couple of examples.

Suppose you are writing a Haskell function `triangle` which is supposed to take an integer, say n, and return the nth triangle number, which is the sum of the first n positive integers. Making use of Haskell's ability to use [1..] to represent the unbounded list of natural numbers 1, 2, 3, 4, ..., you might first write:

Haskell example (don't do this!)

```
triangle :: Integer -> Integer
triangle n = sum (take n [1..])
```

but you would get a compile-time error

```
take.hs:2:24: error:
   - Couldn't match expected type 'Int' with actual type 'Integer'
   - In the first argument of 'take', namely 'n'
     In the first argument of 'sum', namely '(take n [1 .. ])'
     In the expression: sum (take n [1 .. ])
   |
2  | triangle n = sum (take n [1..])
   |                         ^
```

This tells you that the function take expects an argument of type Int, while you are giving it an argument of type Integer. Most likely, the root cause of the error is that you did not realise Haskell has two different integer types, one for machine integers and one for arbitrary precision arithmetic: but this is easy to look up, once you read the error message.

Another common cause of type errors, in any language, is getting arguments in the wrong order. Suppose you wrote

Haskell example (don't do this!)

```
triangle :: Int -> Int
triangle n = sum (take [1..] n)
```

through mistakenly thinking take wanted its integer argument after its list argument, instead of before. You would get an error "Couldn't match expected type '[Int]' with actual type 'Int'", followed, as before, by exhaustive information about where the problem arose. Once you read that the take function is being given an integer where it expects a list of integers (notated [Int] in Haskell), it is the work of a moment to swap the arguments.

Haskell example

```
triangle :: Int -> Int
triangle n = sum (take n [1..])
```

It may help you in future if you also take a moment to think about *why* the arguments are in that order. In this case, it is syntactically convenient to have the list come last, because this makes it easier to use `take` in contexts where a list is repeatedly processed, in a pipeline, by many functions. Even if you do not come up with an explanation, having thought about it may help you to remember the argument order!

> ### Is it the compiler that's wrong?
>
> No. Well, almost certainly no. After twenty-five years of teaching programming, on and off, I recently had a case where a first-year undergraduate student had a problem understanding a compiler's error message and it *did* turn out to be a (known) compiler bug. However, I've lost track of how many times new students have suspected a compiler bug that wasn't there. Unless you just wrote the compiler – in which case you're not what I mean by a "new student" anyway – assume it is correct.

9.2 When Your Program Runs but Behaves Wrongly

Suppose your code compiles and runs – but it doesn't do what you expect. Perhaps it yields a wrong result, causes confusing behaviour of some interface, or prints something you don't expect; perhaps it even crashes or seems to run for ever. What then?

The first thing is to look for the simplest case where the program doesn't do the right thing. Preferably, write an automated test that fails, exercising your program in this simplest case: but if you are not yet writing automated tests, making a note, and running the test manually, will do for now. Getting this test to pass is a concrete goal to aim for. As mentioned in Chapter 7, keeping it in the set of tests that you run regularly in future will ensure that you do not re-introduce the same bug, that is, it will prevent *regression*.

Once you have that simplest case, commit to fixing the bug in that case before you worry about any other case. You need to understand what your program does in this case, and how it's different from what you want. Perhaps there is a problem with the flow of control, e.g. because you have got the wrong expression in an if statement so a section of code gets executed when it should not, for example; or perhaps your code sets a value that is not the one you intended. Whatever the issue is, you need to look in detail at what your program does – concretely, in this simplest buggy case – to find out precisely where, and how, something goes wrong.

Inserting Print Statements

This is usually the easiest way to proceed. Probably – at least if you are using an imperative language – you will have been taught how to print a string to the console (to "standard out", abbreviated "stdout") early in your course. You can use that to help understand what's going on. For example, if you have written some code which you think should do the right thing, but it doesn't seem to be working, is that code section ever run? Or is there some earlier problem that means the computer doesn't ever reach that section of code? You can find out by putting a print statement at the beginning of the section, e.g.

```
print("Got here!")
```

Doing this also helps to detect a surprisingly common problem: when the version of your program that you are *editing* is not the same version that you are *running*.

If you start to suspect that some value is incorrect, print it out at key points and see.

This approach is crude, but often effective. Don't forget to remove the print statements once you are confident that the aspect of behaviour they are checking is correct, otherwise your output becomes cluttered and confusing.

Logging

A less crude alternative to using print statements is to use a logging framework, such as Log4j in Java or logger in Python. Such frameworks have a learning curve, but once learned, they give you an easy way to turn all your debugging messages on, or off, together.

Interactive Debugging

Sometimes understanding your bug is easiest if you can interact with the program from the inside, rather than running it as though you were a normal user of the program. For example, if there is a function which, in normal operation, is called by another part of your program, with a complex argument, you may want to call it manually with a simple argument, or with a succession of different arguments, to clarify whether it does what it should. If you have an interactive prompt, you may be able to load your program at the prompt, and have considerable freedom to explore. This is the commonest way to debug Haskell code. It is also possible, although not quite so convenient, in Python (using the `code` module).

A more sophisticated approach, requiring a little more investment up front but with the potential to save you time in the long run, is to use a *debugger*.

A debugger is a specific program whose aim is, as the name suggests, to help you get rid of bugs. Most languages have debuggers available, but they're often not taught in beginners' programming courses, because they can be quite forbidding at first. A debugger might be a standalone tool, or might be built into your IDE if you're using one.

The basic features you need to be able to use are:

• setting a *breakpoint* – that is, arranging that every time the flow of control gets to a certain line, the execution will stop, so that you can try:

- *single-stepping* – that is, letting the program execute one line at a time, e.g. so that you can check which way it goes at an `if` statement; or
- examining the values of variables.

A little exploration of the interface will probably reveal how to use these. Many debuggers have lots of more sophisticated features, but you don't need them for now. When you do feel like investigating, see if there's a tutorial for the specific debugger you're using.

To get maximum benefit, you need to learn not just the mechanics of using a debugger, but also how to use a debugger effectively. Forming a hypothesis first, and then testing it, is a useful technique here. For example, if you are about to step through a line that calculates a value, *first* ask yourself what you expect the value to be, *then* do the step and check whether it is. If you just wait for something surprising to happen, it's remarkably easy not to notice where the trouble begins. It's fine, of course, to run the debugger several times, first to get an overview of what's happening, and then, more carefully, to understand important sections of it in detail.

Changing the Program to Understand It

What can you do if you can neither find a usable debugger, nor get your program to print an informative string when it gets to an informative place in the computation? You could consider rewriting it into more inspectable pieces, to understand what's going on.

We are not talking, here, about the kind of restructuring that improves your program overall. This is not a good time to undertake that kind of work: since you are starting with a program whose behaviour you don't fully understand, changing it radically may leave you more confused. It is better to make minimal, careful changes at this stage, and accept that you may need to undo them after you have understood the bug. For example, if you have an encapsulated (hidden) function which you suspect may be the cause of the problem, make a copy of it that's out in the open, and try it out separately.

Suppose you are trying to debug this function, which, let's say, is part of an exercise about decoding a ciphertext.

Haskell example

```
possibilities :: String -> [(Int, String)]
possibilities str
  = [(i, rotate i str) | i <- [0..25], isPossible (rotate i str)]
    where isPossible str = str == "AND" && str == "THE"
```

It calls on another function `rotate`, which we'll suppose you're not suspicious of. `rotate` replaces each character in a string by the character that is a given number of places away in the alphabet, e.g. `rotate 1 "CAT"` will return `"DBU"`, because D is 1 place after C in the alphabet, etc.. The `possibilities` function is supposed to test each possible rotation value, from 0 to 25, on a given string, and keep the rotation value and resulting string only if the decoded version is "AND" or "THE". You can probably immediately see the problem, but suppose, for a moment, that you couldn't. You look at the first line of the `possibilities` definition, and it seems to be OK …but there's still a bug; even when you run `possibilities` on the plain string "AND", it returns an empty list of possibilities! You finally suspect that the problem is the `isPossible` function, but it's late and you stare at it without seeing a problem. If only you could test `isPossible` separately … but it's encapsulated inside the definition of possibilities.

Just fix it so that it isn't, then:

Haskell example

```
isPossible str = str == "AND" && str == "THE"

possibilities :: String -> [(Int, String)]
possibilities str
  = [(i, rotate i str) | i <- [0..25], isPossible (rotate i str)]
```

Now isPossible is a top-level function, like possibilities itself, and you can test it as such. You'll quickly see that isPossible "AND" returns false, and hopefully from there it's a short step to noticing the && that should be ||.

Once you have understood and fixed the problem, return the function to its proper place! It was encapsulated for good reason: so that it cannot be called outside the possibilities function, and hence cannot contribute to any bug outside it.

Another situation in which you may need to change your program in order to understand – not fix – the bug is where your code relies on code you did not write, and you want to understand whereabouts in the interaction the problem lies. Our next story is about such a case.

Story

Kasia is working on a Java exercise where she was given some of the code for an object that moves a sprite on her screen, and has to write a few more methods for it. The code she's been given uses some other code files that she's also been given, but isn't expected to change. She's done several parts successfully, but in this one, what she sees on her screen isn't what she expects. The new code that she's just written (inside a loop which we don't show) looks like this:

Java example (don't do this!)

```
move(4);
if (froboz.getRandomNumber(100) < 10);
{
    turn(froboz.getRandomNumber(45) + 20);
}
```

and she's not at all sure what the problem is. Has she misunderstood how `froboz`, which is one of the objects she's been given, is supposed to work? Has she got the wrong bound for the choice of random number? Is she starting at the wrong position on the screen? Or what?

The first thing she decides to rule in or out is that the random numbers she's getting are somehow not what she expects. She decides to investigate the case where the first random number turns out to be 5 and the second one to be 30. So she changes the code to:

Java example (don't do this!)

```java
move(4);
if (5 < 10);
{
    turn(30 + 20);
}
```

She finds that the behaviour of the sprite doesn't change much, so she tries the case where the first random number is large. She also decides she understands how < and + work so she simplifies the code further for this case:

Java example (don't do this!)

```java
move(4);
if (false);
{
    turn(50);
}
```

She expects no turning to happen at all this time – after all, if (false) should never evaluate to true, so the turning should never happen, she thinks. To her surprise, the behaviour of her sprite still doesn't seem to change at all. Next she tries commenting out each line in turn to see what effect that has. She can stop the sprite moving or turning by commenting out the relevant line – but commenting out the if line doesn't seem to make any difference. Puzzled, she compares her code with an example in her Java textbook, and notices (what you may have noticed long ago) that the examples there don't have semi-colons after their if (condition) parts like she does. Hmm, she had thought you always had to have a semi-colon at the end of a line – and surely, she thinks, if having a semi-colon were an error, her code wouldn't have compiled, so it can't be that – this must be one of those cases where you can include a thing or not and it makes no difference? Just for thoroughness, she tries removing the semi-colon in her original code anyway, and miraculously, it works.

She shows her dedication to becoming a good programmer in what she does next. Instead of just going on with the exercise, she decides to take a few minutes to understand what was happening. Why does removing her semi-colon fix her problem? She decides to investigate semi-colons after ifs in a separate, free-standing program that isn't complicated by any of the sprite stuff. Here it is:

Java example (don't do this!)

```java
public class IfFalse {
  public static void main(String[] args) {
    if (false);
    {
      System.out.println("yay,_got_here!");
    }
  }
}
```

After playing with this she goes back to her Java textbook and spends a bit of time on the web reading about blocks and empty statements, and ends up understanding a lot more about the role of semi-colons in Java than she did to start with.

Notice that we didn't say much about exactly how what Kasia saw differed from what she expected. That's because in this fictitious case, she didn't analyse that much. A different approach would have been not to alter the code at all, but instead, to watch very carefully what happened and think about the relationship with the code. Perhaps by doing that Kasia could have realised that her turn command was always being executed, not only on some randomly chosen occasions. However, depending on how complicated the rest of the behaviour of the system was, and especially on how much randomness there was in it, that might have been harder than what she did.

9.2.1 Special Cases: Non-termination and Crashes

When Your Program Runs for Ever You start your program, expecting it to run for a moment and give a result, and instead, it runs but does not terminate. Either nothing visible happens, or you have an endless stream of output. You will need to stop the program manually, either by pressing the appropriate button in your IDE, or by using the operating system directly, e.g. hitting Control-C in a Linux system, or killing the command window in which it is running.

Usually this is a sign that your program contains an endless loop (or an endless stream of recursive calls). Check the loop conditions, or the logic that leads to recursion, carefully. Ask yourself: why do I expect this process ever to finish? If you do not immediately see the problem – especially if there is more than one loop and you are not sure which one is causing the problem – then either tracing the program execution in a debugger, or inserting print statements, can help you see what is going wrong.

It is possible that what you have is not true non-termination, but a very inefficient program that is doing more work than you expected – it would finish eventually, but not until the middle of next week, or worse. Fortunately such problems are rare in early programming exercise solutions: if you have managed to create one, you probably have a good idea about how. Trying your program on the smallest, simplest input data you can is often a good start.

When Your Program Crashes You start your program, expecting it to run for a moment and give a result, and instead it stops with some kind of error message. Depending on your language this might be an unhandled exception, a segmentation fault, an out of memory error, a stack overflow, or something else. (We will call them all "crashes" in what follows.) The effect is the same: no result, and a possibly cryptic message about what went wrong. You can follow a similar procedure to the one described for compile-time errors, first attempting to get as much information as possible out of the error message, and, if necessary, modifying the program to investigate further. However, since your program does run before it crashes, you also have the option of using a debugger, or print statements, to track down the problem.

Terminology: Null pointer exception

In Java (and related languages such as C and C++), *null pointer exceptions*, abbreviated NPEs, are the commonest cause of crashes. An NPE arises when your code attempts to dereference a reference – we may equivalently say, follow a pointer – whose value is null. What does this mean? A reference (or pointer) is a name which can be used to refer to a piece of state, e.g. an object. To dereference (or follow) it is to use the name to access the state, e.g. send a message to the object. Problems arise if your code does this when, in fact, the reference does not currently name any state at all – that is, when the reference is null. Because nothing sensible can be done – you can't send a message to an object that isn't there – an exception will be raised, and (unless your code also *catches* the exception and does something to recover) your program will crash.

A particularly useful kind of error output that you may see following a crash – but one that beginners often find intimidating, and therefore fail to use to full advantage – is a stack trace.

Terminology: Stack trace

A stack trace is an ordered list of all the methods or functions that the program has entered, but not exited.

The first thing to do is to check that you understand which order the list is given in. The most recently entered function may be at the top (usual in Java) or the bottom (usual in Python). This is the one where the crash occurred. At the other end of the stack trace is whatever function was invoked at the very start of your program's run (e.g. `main`): however, you may not see this, because the stack trace may be abbreviated, only showing the last few functions. Suppose the function where the crash occurred was called `findCustomer`. This is shown at one end of the stack trace, and the line number is the one where the crash occurred. The next line in the list is the function that called `findCustomer`, and the line number shows where `findCustomer` was called, and so on.

Usually the bug is located in the most recent function (`findCustomer` in our example), but not always. Especially, if you see that the most recent calls are not to code you wrote, but to standard library or infrastructure functions, don't be tempted to suspect them! What it probably means is that your code invoked a library function incorrectly, e.g. with invalid arguments, which later caused a problem. Look at the most recent place in the stack trace that is about *your* code, and work from there.

9.3 Cardboard Debugging

This useful technique is known by many names, including for example "rubber duck debugging"; I call it "cardboard debugging" because that's the name I first learned for it – and because no rubber duck manufacturer has made me a tempting sponsorship offer yet.

The key observation is that when you can't understand why your program isn't working, it often helps to explain, in detail, to someone else, why it *should* work. You might, for example, explain it to a peer or to a tutor on your course. However, the next important observation is that when you do this, it will usually be *you*, not the other person, who suddenly sees what the problem is. It turns out that it doesn't matter much whether the other person was following your explanation – or even was capable of following your explanation. The logical conclusion, which, surprisingly, turns out to hold, is that it is almost as effective to explain your program to a cardboard cutout of your tutor – or even to an *imaginary* cardboard cutout of your tutor – as to your real-life tutor. You'll feel daft, but give it a go.

9.4 If All Else Fails

Sometimes, however, you find the only sensible reaction to your problem is "don't start from here". If trying to localise and understand your bug reveals to you that your program is a horrible mess that you can't understand, you could consider:

- starting again from scratch, this time testing as you go (see Chapter 7) and keeping your program clear (Chapter 8);
- refactoring (more on how to do this in Chapter 10).

> **Terminology: Refactoring**
>
> To *refactor* a program is to change it without changing its functionality. You might do this to make the program easier to understand or easier to change.

   This is not the ideal time for refactoring – ideally, you would start with a program *you* completely understood, but wanted to improve, e.g. to make it easier for *other people*, or yourself at a later date, to understand – but sometimes it may be the best of a bad bunch of options. When I have lost a thing, and have failed to find it in the first few places I look, I often take this as a sign that I need to calm down and tidy up generally. Almost always, this is as efficient as any other way of finding the lost item, and it improves my environment as well. Sometimes the analogous strategy works in programming.

Tip

If what you have is a mess of spaghetti code that doesn't work, any way of recovering is going to feel challenging. Don't despair, it happens to pretty much every beginning programmer some time, and motivates the development of good habits to stop it happening again! Do consider getting a cup of coffee at this stage, or going for a walk, or even getting some sleep and coming back to the problem when you're rested.

9.5 Removing the Bug

Most bugs are blessedly easy to remove, once you fully understand what and where they are.

Tip

Even if, in the course of localising your bug, you make a change to the program that seems to make it go away, make sure you fully understand, before you move on.

One reason for this tip is that the process of understanding a bug, especially in code you wrote, is usually educational. Does the existence of the bug point at something you do not quite understand about the language? Regard your bug as a learning opportunity, and get all the value you can from it. For example, in our Haskell example, a poor way to use the bug arising from a use of Integer where Int was expected would be just to see that the error message says something about Int and change Integer to Int; a better way is to look up the difference between Integer and Int and understand it once and for all. If Kasia in our story earlier had moved on as soon as she observed that deleting the semi-colon fixed her problem, she might have ended up with a confused feeling that semi-colons were sometimes problematic. Such lurking confusions sap your confidence.

Another reason is that the bug is not the same thing as the indicator that told you there was a bug. If you edit the program without fully understanding what the problem was, you may make the indicator go away, without having fixed the real problem. You may then have a program that still has a bug, but has a different, less natural one that will be harder to debug when it does eventually come to light. For example, in Python, suppose you had written

Python example

```python
def get_data(file_name):
    with open(file_name) as file:
        data = file.read()
        # etc: code to work with the data...
```

and everything was going well, until you accidentally called the function with a file name that did not exist. At this point, an exception (a FileNotFoundError) would be raised. You *could* modify the code to this:

Python example (don't do this!)

```python
def get_data(file_name):
    try:
        with open(file_name) as file:
            data = file.read()
            # etc: code to work with the data...
    except:
        pass
```

which has the effect of making the function do nothing at all, not even complain, if the file does not exist. The symptom, namely the raised exception, goes away. However, this is a **REALLY BAD IDEA**. The next time the function is called on a non-existent file name, you may be much further on with your development, and it may be less obvious to you what has happened. Perhaps some code far away in your program will mysteriously fail, and the root cause may be hard to determine. Instead, handle the error condition in whatever way is sensible in the context, perhaps by printing or logging an error message, and stopping the program if it will not make sense to continue.

Often you will eventually realise that your program was doing what you intended it to do, but that your intention was wrong – there was a bug in your understanding of the task. The example at the start of Chapter 8 was a case in point: probably the student who wrote the "bad" version had not realised that the code was supposed to do nothing at all, if given an argument other than 12, 15 or 18.

Sometimes, once you fix your understanding of the problem, you realise that your program can't possibly do what it needs to do: your misunderstanding influenced something basic about how you wrote the code. In such cases, you may need to do something more like starting again from scratch. But keep a copy of your buggy code, in case you can save time by pasting in chunks of it that *do* turn out to be part of what you want!

9.6 After Removing the Bug

In order to wring as much value as you can out of your debugging effort, ask yourself, before you move on:

1. Might there be another similar bug in this program? How can I check?

2. How did I come to introduce this bug? How can I avoid doing so in future?

Let's look at these issues in turn.

9.6.1 Finding Similar Bugs

Some bugs will be really specific to one setting, but many will not be. For example, here's a classic:

Java example (don't do this!)

```
// boolean found says whether we've found something yet
if (found = false) {
  // we haven't found it yet: keep searching...
}
```

Stop here and see if you can see the problem. (It's possible that in your language this code is correct, but the problem exists not only in Java but also in Python, C and C++, among others, so it's worth learning about it anyway.) Got it?

The problem is that in the `if` statement, the programmer intends to compare `found` with `false`. However, in Java (and many other languages), the correct syntax for that uses a double equals sign, `==`, not the single `=` we see here.[1] The compiler didn't complain, because the version with `=` does make sense – just not the sense the programmer intended. What it does is to assign `false` as the new value of `found`.

---

1 But there are languages – notably BASIC and its relatives – that use the same syntax for comparison and assignment, distinguishing them by context. If you learned such a language first, you will have to be *especially* careful when you learn a language that uses different syntax for the two ideas.

Tip

Never, ever compare boolean variables with literal true and false values. Instead of if (found == true), just write if (found). It means the same, is shorter and clearer, and doesn't run the risk of writing = where you meant ==. Similarly, instead of if (found == false), write if (!found) (using whatever the syntax is, in your language, for the negation of the boolean variable found).

   This tip applies in every[a] programming language – if it's valid to write a boolean expression (such as found == true) in some context, it will be valid to write a plain boolean (such as found). Try it!

---

a I don't often make claims as bold as that! If you know an exception, let me know.

We have identified two different problems:

1. Use of = (assignment) when == (comparison for equality) was intended.
2. Comparison of a boolean variable with true or false.

The first will give you wrong results, while the second is "only" bad style. Both are easy to eliminate, so if you find you have one instance of either, do a search and see if there are any more instances. Similarly, each time you find a bug in your program, take a moment to think about whether there could be other, similar, bugs, that you should find and destroy.

9.6.2 Avoiding Ever Introducing That Bug Again

It's tempting just to decide to "try harder" not to introduce bugs, but human brains will make mistakes. Make peace with yours, and instead of expecting perfection from it, try to establish habits that will support you in writing correct code.

Curiously, simply knowing that you sometimes introduce a certain kind of bug will help you to avoid doing so. At least subconsciously, you will have a mental inventory of things to look out for, when you scan a chunk of code to check it's what you intended, or when something isn't working as you expect. Your checking may be more reliable if you make this inventory explicit in the form of a checklist. It might include, for example:

- Are all names that appear in the specification exactly correct?
- Are all loop bounds correct?
- Are array sizes correct?
- Are all array indexes correct?
- Do I check for errors, or handle exceptions, arising from code I call?
- Do I have any null pointer errors (dereferencing things that might be null)?
- Do loops and recursions always terminate as they should?
- …

> **Tip**
>
> Consider keeping such a checklist, and each time you remove a bug, think about whether there is something you should add to the list.

Sometimes you may be able to adopt a coding habit that will help you to avoid certain kinds of bugs. Let us consider some common bugs and how to avoid them, in more detail.

Avoiding Non-termination If your language offers you a choice of `for` loops and `while` loops, you should usually prefer `for` loops. This may seem counter-intuitive, as `while` loops are at least as powerful: it is always possible to rewrite code that uses a `for` loop so that it uses a `while` loop instead.[2] However, a common bug is *accidental non-termination*: when a loop, that should be executed only a finite number of times, is repeated for ever. In practice you are more likely to introduce this bug into a `while` loop than into the equivalent `for` loop. Why is this? It is because the syntax of the `for` loop explicitly shows the loop variable, which is changed each time you go round the loop, and the finite set it runs over. For example:

Python example

```python
for i in range(0, 5):
    # do some things...
    # i is never changed inside the loop
```

By contrast, in a `while` loop you have to manage the change yourself in code that is inside the loop. Here is the `while` equivalent of the `for` loop above:

Python example

```python
i = 0
while (i < 5):
    # do some things...
    i += 1
```

`while` loops are convenient when, at the time of entering the loop, it is not possible to know – to write an expression for – how many times the loop should be iterated. For example, here is some code that finds the highest power of 2 that divides an integer, `composite`:

---

2 In Java, and many other languages, you can also always rewrite code that uses a `while` loop to use a `for` loop instead, so the two kinds of loop are formally interchangeable.

Python example

```python
n = composite
power = 0
while (n % 2 == 0):
    power += 1
    n /= 2
print("2_to_the_power", power, "divides", composite)
```

This extra flexibility can be very useful, but if you don't need it, then it is just an opportunity to forget to change your loop variable.

Tip

Use `for` unless there is a good reason why you need the flexibility of `while`.

A habit that may prevent you from accidentally writing non-terminating `while` loops is to document *why* the loop should terminate, in a comment. What you write does not have to be super-formal to be valuable. In the last example, you might write "n halves until it is odd".

Similar considerations apply to recursive code: if you write code that may call itself, and you expect it to terminate, you must think about how you know that it will. Here is a Haskell equivalent of the last example:

Haskell example

```haskell
powerOf2In :: Integer -> Integer
powerOf2In n | n `mod` 2 > 0 = 0
             | otherwise = 1 + (powerOf2In (n `div` 2))
```

In this recursive code, we explicitly give the base case: that is, there is a line of code to say what happens when we cannot divide n by 2 any more, because it is odd. This style may help you to think about termination. It does not guarantee that your base case will ever be reached, however – you still have to think about that!

Avoiding Null Pointer Exceptions When your code accepts a reference, there may be no alternative to checking (e.g. using an `isNull` function) that it is not null, before you *dereference* it – that is, use it to access what it points at. Occasionally, though, you can avoid the risk of dereferencing it, using a trick such as this one: when you want to compare a known object, such as a literal string, with an object that might be null, call the `equals` method on the known object:

Java example

```
// String s might be null
s.equals("foo"); // might give NPE
"foo".equals(s); // may look odd, but cannot give NPE
```

To help yourself and anyone else who writes code that interacts with yours, when you write methods that return objects, document whether they might, or will never, return `null`. As a matter of style, prefer to write methods that guarantee not to return `null` when you have a choice. You might like to look up how to use *annotations* such as `@NotNull`, which can also help.

Avoiding Off-by-one Errors These can occur in any programming language.

Terminology: Off-by-One error

An *off-by-one error* is a bug in the logic of a program, where some numeric value differs, by one, from a correct value.

A common cause is writing $<$ where you meant $\leq$ or similar, which is particularly often a problem in loop bounds. Where you can, iterate over a collection, rather than using a loop variable that you do not need. For example, in Java this:

Java example

```java
for (String s : args)
{
  // things that use s
}
```

is safer than this:

Java example

```java
for (int i = 0; i < args.length; i++)
{
  String s = args[i];
  // things that use s
}
```

because if there is no integer i in the code you cannot do the wrong thing with it! As with the discussion of for versus while loops, the safer version is less flexible; sometimes you will need access to an explicit loop variable. Make a habit, though, of using the safer version unless you need the flexibility.

Off-by-one errors can also arise when you index into arrays or lists. In many languages the first element of an array is at index 0, not index 1, which can take a while to get used to after a lifetime of counting from 1!

Avoiding Accidental Assignment Finally let us return to the =/== problem which we considered earlier. Here's a trick that some

people like. When you want to compare things, it'll often be the
case that one of them is a thing you can assign to, and one of them
isn't. For example, in Java you might write

```
x = 0
```

but you can't write

```
0 = x
```

because 0 is a constant. You can use this fact to your advantage,
by making a habit of writing constants on the left-hand side of
comparisons. If you miss out one of the equals signs in

```
x == 0
```

you will get code that makes sense, but does not do what you
intended. If, on the other hand, you accidentally miss out one of
the equals signs in

```
0 == x
```

the compiler will point out your mistake, because `0 = x` isn't valid
code.

9.6.3 Defensive Programming

Suppose you are writing a function which takes an integer argument, and you believe the caller of your function ought to ensure
that the integer they pass in is positive. Perhaps you believe this
because the expectation has been made explicit in a *pre-condition*,
as discussed in Chapter 8. If you nevertheless check it as the
first thing your function does, this is an example of *defensive
programming*: you are defending against the possibility that the
caller makes a mistake.

Terminology: Defensive programming

Defensive programming is a general term for any programming
technique that minimises the harm done by a bug, or any other
unforeseen circumstance.

By programming defensively, you ensure that you cannot be blamed for a problem that is not your fault. If you check a precondition and complain immediately if your code is being called with arguments it should not have to handle, you avoid the risk that your code malfunctions on the argument it was not designed to handle and somebody later blames you for this. Of course, often you will be the author of both caller and callee, in which case the benefit to you is that defensive programming makes it easier to identify where a problem begins.

More generally, what you need to defend against, and how, depends on the circumstances. Sometimes – for example, in many safety-critical situations – it is important to enable the program to keep running, even if something unexpected happens; you might supply sensible default values for missing data, for example, in order to defend against the program crashing or showing unpredictable behaviour. At other times, it is better to stop the program immediately a problem occurs, emitting a useful diagnostic message; this defends against hard-to-track-down misbehaviour that the problem might cause later.

Students often worry that by inserting checks that shouldn't really be necessary because they should always succeed (if everything else in the program is correct), they are bloating their programs and making them inefficient. Don't worry about this. Most such checks are very quick, and modern compilers are pretty good at optimising out checks that are truly unnecessary. Human brain power is a much more limited resource, and that's what you should be trying to save.

That said, if you, and every other reader of the code, can *easily and confidently* see that a check is not required, then there is no virtue in including it. This is a kind of code sense.

10

How to Improve Your Program

We have talked about how to debug your program (Chapter 9) and about the basics of making your program clear and readable (Chapter 8). What else could we mean by "improving" your program?

We're touching here on *design*. In software engineering, design is about building software that not only meets the requirements, but does so in the best possible way. There are many ways we can judge how good a design is. Two of them are:

* how *maintainable* your program is;
* how *efficient* your program is.

Let's discuss these aspects in turn, and then we'll discuss how you can get to there from here. That is, if your program works, but you decide it could, and should, be more maintainable or more efficient, how can you safely improve it, without breaking it in the process? To do that you use the technique (briefly mentioned in Chapter 9) called *refactoring*.

10.1 Maintainability

A very reasonable first reaction to coming across the idea of a program being maintainable is confusion. Lines of code don't wear out and need retyping – semi-colons don't drop off the ends from time to time – so what are we talking about? The term *maintenance* has stuck since the early days of programming, and probably came in by analogy with manufacturing physical goods. The thing being maintained is not really the program, but the *relationship* between the program and its environment, which includes the people, processes, software and hardware that the program must interact with. Whenever something in the environment changes, the program may need to change, in order to maintain the relationship. For example, it's normal to have to change a program from time to time to keep track of new versions of the programming language. It's even more common for the needs of the users to change over time. Stretching the definition, even fixing bugs can be seen as a kind of maintenance. The easier it is to effect any necessary changes, the more maintainable we say your program is.

When you're new to programming, especially in the artificial setting of a beginners' programming course, you are relatively isolated from these concerns. Most likely, you'll be given a clearly described problem to solve, and nothing about it will change while you do it. Even so, thinking about maintainability is a good habit to get into, because the same properties that make code easy to maintain also help to get it correct.

The first stage of ensuring maintainability is following the guidelines we discussed in Chapter 8 for making your program clear. That's because any kind of maintenance to a program involves someone being able to understand how it works *now*, so that they can confidently change it. If your program is difficult to understand, they may find themselves guessing about what the program currently does, or about what it is supposed to do, which makes the process of changing it less reliable.

> **Tip**
>
> Even if you are confident you are the only person who will ever need to change your program, it still pays to work on its clarity. You might be surprised by how fast you forget what was in your head when you wrote it!

The next stage of ensuring maintainability is to think about what changes are most likely to be required in future, and structure the program so as to make those changes as easy as possible. This may sound as though it requires a crystal ball, and indeed it is not always easy. You may guess that if your program talks about three kinds of widget, then it is quite likely that a fourth kind of widget might be required in future. Whether that is really true, though, is not something you can work out just by looking at your program: it depends on the real world.

10.1.1 Eliminating Duplication

> **The "Write Once!" rule**
>
> The idea is that each thing – let's say, each independent decision – ought to be incorporated just once into the program. That way, if this decision needs to be changed later, there is only one place in the program that needs to be changed. This is easier than changing several places, and avoids the risk that you accidentally miss out one of the places that should be changed.

This is not precise – it is only a rule of thumb – because it is not always obvious what constitutes a "thing" that should be recorded just once. Some cases are very clear. Suppose a large chunk of code is repeated, exactly, three times in your program, and under all circumstances that you can imagine, any change that had to be made to one of the copies would have to be made to all three. Then the decisions incorporated in that code are written three times, for no good reason. You should definitely look for a way to remove the duplication, perhaps by making the chunk of code into the body of a function that can be called three times.

However, with smaller chunks of code it becomes important to ask yourself whether they will really always be the same – they record the same decision – or whether they just happen to be the same at the moment.

Here's a simple example.

Java example (before refactoring)

```java
if (noItems > 10) {
  basketKind = "big";
  sorted = 1;
} else if (noItems > 5) {
  basketKind = "medium";
  sorted = 1;
} else {
  basketKind = "small";
  sorted = 1;
}
```

There are quite a few things wrong with this! Rather than fix them all at once, though, we pick one aspect to improve first. Here we see that one line,

```java
sorted = 1;
```

occurs three times. Suppose that, in context, we understand that this genuinely is duplication of a decision: if one of these lines changed (say, we changed sorted to decided, or we changed its type to boolean so that it would have to be set to true instead of to 1), all three would have to change. We can change the code to have that line only once, without changing anything about how it behaves. This is an example of a refactoring. Here's the code after that one change.

```java
if (noItems > 10) {
  basketKind = "big";
} else if (noItems > 5) {
  basketKind = "medium";
} else {
  basketKind = "small";
}
sorted = 1;
```

The second version looks neater and is shorter – but that isn't really the point. The point is that it no longer contains the same line of code several times. Now if we decide to change the name or type of the variable `sorted`, we only have to change it in one place, not several. That's quicker and easier, and, even more importantly, we're more likely to get it right. Bugs that are introduced by changing one copy of some duplicated code but not another copy are a real pain, and we can avoid them by avoiding duplicating code.

Tip

A word of warning: while eliminating duplicate code is often useful, you should be cautious if you find yourself getting too proud of how short your program is. In many cases, a shorter program can be *less* maintainable than a longer one, because it can be harder to understand, and dependencies between its parts may be more intricate.

Consider the following example of a solution to the Fizz Buzz problem, in Haskell. It is the shortest we have seen yet – but you will have to be quite a Haskell wizard to understand how it works, and even so, how long does it take you?

Haskell example

```
main :: IO ()
main = h (zipWith3 g (f 3 "Fizz") (f 5 "Buzz") [1..100])
  where
    f n s = cycle (replicate (n-1) "" ++ [s])
    g s t n = head (filter (not . null) [s ++ t, show n])
    h = putStr . unlines
```

Now, how about this, only slightly longer, version?

Haskell example

```
say :: Integer -> String
say i | (i `mod` 3 == 0) && (i `mod` 5 == 0) = "FizzBuzz"
      | i `mod` 3 == 0 = "Fizz"
      | i `mod` 5 == 0 = "Buzz"
      | otherwise = show i

main :: IO()
main = putStr $ unlines $ map say [1..100]
```

Even if you are not learning Haskell, you can see how the structure of the second version matches the structure of the problem. The function say computes the string that should result from a single integer; then these results are put together in main.

Magic constants

A *magic constant* is a literal value that occurs in your program. Examples include 3, 5, "Fizz" and "Buzz" in our Fizz Buzz

programs, and the special threshold values 5 and 10 for
noItems in the Java example we just saw.

It is often – but not always! – better to replace these literal
values by named constants, which are assigned values elsewhere
in the program. Our Java example might become

```
if (noItems > LARGE_NUMBER_OF_ITEMS) {
  basketKind = "big";
} else if (noItems > MEDIUM_NUMBER_OF_ITEMS) {
  basketKind = "medium";
} else {
  basketKind = "small";
}
sorted = 1;
```

This is arguably clearer, but it is less self-contained: to understand it fully, you have to look up the values of those constants.
Here are some factors to bear in mind as you think about
the costs and benefits of replacing a literal value by a named
constant.

• How often is the literal value used (for exactly the same
  purpose, so that changing one instance of it would definitely require changing all of them) in the program? The
  more often it is used – especially if the uses are widely
  spread in the program – the more you will gain from using
  a named constant instead; you will be reducing the risk
  that someone accidentally changes some but not all of the
  instances.
• How likely is it that the literal value will have to be changed?
  The more likely it is, the more you might gain by using a

named constant, whose value could be changed just once, where it is defined. On the other extreme, most programs will use the literal value 0 in roles where it will definitely never change; there is nothing to be gained from replacing these uses by a named constant.

- Can you give the constant a name which will explain why this literal value is used? If so, using a named constant may make the code easier to understand. For example, DAYS_IN_WEEK might sometimes give more readable code than 7.
- Can you give the constant a name which will minimise copying errors? For example, rather than repeatedly using 3.1415926535, using the named constant PI saves programmers from typos and from using inconsistent precision.

Do not mechanically use a named constant to replace every literal value in your program: do so only when the benefit is worth the cost.

10.1.2 Choice of Abstraction

Software design is largely about choosing a good *structure* for your program. For example, you might introduce a subroutine, which you call multiple times, to avoid duplicating code.

Abstraction is more than this, though. Choosing a set of abstractions is about providing a conceptual way in to your program: you identify certain things that the reader should focus on, and you choose those things carefully to be the things they need to know about, and need to use, in order to understand the program and make foreseeable changes to it. The collection of names in your program should constitute a usable vocabulary for talking about what the program does in the world.

For example, it can be useful to separate some lines of code off into a new function. This can be worthwhile even if that function will be called only once, if you can give the function a good name that explains what it does. The reason is that if you, or someone else, come along later looking for a bug in the code, you may be able to avoid looking at those lines of code, if you're confident that the problem is nothing to do with that aspect of what the program does. You're saying something like: the reader needs to know that there is a function called this, but they probably don't need to look at the details of what it does: they can simply assume that the name is a reasonable description.

Suppose at some early stage of doing an exercise, you have this code:

Python example (before refactoring)

```python
def total(basket, country):
    total = 0
    for item in basket:
        total += price(item)
    if total > 10: #free shipping offer
        return total
    if country == "UK" and weight(basket) <= 1:
        total += STANDARD_UK_SHIPPING
    else:
        raise NotImplementedError
    return total
```

The program isn't finished, as we see from the NotImplementedError: it raises an exception when circumstances arise that it cannot yet deal with. However, it is already getting to be a bit of a mess. Perhaps before you go on to handle the other cases, you might refactor the program into:

Python example (after refactoring)

```python
def total(basket, country):
    total = basket_total(basket)
    if total > 10:  #free shipping offer
        shipping = 0
    else:
        shipping = shipping_cost(basket, country)
    return total + shipping

def basket_total(basket):
    return sum (price(item) for item in basket)

def shipping_cost(basket, country):
    if country == "UK" and weight(basket) <= 1:
        return STANDARD_UK_SHIPPING
    else:
        raise NotImplementedError
```

The functionality is the same, but in the second case, we have split independent chunks of what the function needs to do into separate, named functions. If there is a problem with, or a change required to, how a shipping cost is calculated, you expect to look at the shipping_cost function and ignore the basket_total function. Even though the code isn't finished, it is worth doing such rewriting as we go. For example, focusing on the code that computes the total of the item prices (basket_total) prompted us into writing that in a more Pythonic way.

A rule of thumb is to try to maximise the probability that the things that have to change will be close together in the program. An important reason for the success of *object-oriented programming* is that the structural chunks of the program often correspond to real-world objects. These are not necessarily physically real things, but they are *domain concepts*: things that have meaning to the customer, so that they are referred to by nouns, such as Account, Customer, Transaction. A set of changes in the real world, which causes changes in the program, is likely to centre around one domain concept. Because the code that corresponds to this concept is all in one chunk of the program, the chances are good that we only have to modify that one chunk. By contrast, if we structure the program according to the steps of what it has to do, it's more likely that several steps, each using that same domain concept, all have to change.

> **Tip**
>
> Choosing good names for chunks of your program can drive the process of improving its structure. For example, if you find it difficult to name a function because it does two unrelated things, split the function into two, each with a good name.

When you look at a program and see that all its names are perfectly apt, and yet quite short, it is tempting to think that the programmer was lucky. Fancy finding that the domain concepts were so easy to describe clearly and concisely, you may think! In fact, it may be that what you are seeing is the end point of a process of improvement. Perhaps the programmer chose maximally descriptive names, even if they were long, and then looked at the over-long names as a sign that the structure of the program was not yet ideal. Refactoring – e.g. splitting non-cohesive units, or pulling out common superclasses or repeated subroutines – then enabled the improvement of the names. For a fuller discussion on using good naming to drive the process of design improvement, see J. B. Rainsberger's blog (Rainsberger, 2013).

10.2 **Efficiency**

A large and challenging part of computer science relates to minimising the computational resources required to carry out some calculation.

Terminology: Moore's Law

Moore's Law is the empirical observation, first made by Gordon Moore in 1965, that the number of transistors on a chip seemed to double every year.

Moore's Law has had many variants: the details do not matter so much as the essence, which is exponential growth in computing power (since, roughly, the number of transistors controls how much computation the chip can do in a given time). Although stories about the end of Moore's Law are becoming increasingly common, the landscape of software engineering, so far, has been shaped by this reality: that computers get better much faster than our ability to program them does. One effect is that computer scientists think in terms of "big O".[1] It is usually not worth a programmer spending a lot of effort working out how to make a program run twice as fast, or in half as much memory: if that is all that is needed, buying a better computer is cheaper than paying the programmer.

Story

Early in my time as a professional software developer, I had to learn Perl, and I did so with the help of the "pink camel book", which was the first edition of *Programming Perl*. (It was so

---

1 If you don't yet know what that means, it doesn't matter: the next sentence gives the rough idea. If you are doing a computer science degree, you probably soon will know.

called because it was pink, and had a camel on the front; sadly, the camel itself was not pink.) In the back of this book was a section about how to write efficient programs in Perl, which made a deep impression on me because it helped me make sense of some arguments between more experienced colleagues.

Its point was that there are many different kinds of efficiency we might aim for. The two that people usually think about are *time efficiency*, which is about making your program run as fast as possible, and *space efficiency*, which is about how to make it run using as small an amount of memory as possible. However, in practice, the things you do to increase those two kinds of efficiency can be in conflict: for example, you might make your program faster by caching some intermediate results, which makes it use more memory. So far so pedestrian. The mind-blowing part was that it also identified – as the best kind of joke, the kind with a serious point – several other kinds of efficiency, such as "programmer efficiency", which is about not wasting your time and effort, and "user efficiency", which is about not wasting the time and effort of the people who will use your program. It pointed out that the phenomenon of reducing one kind of efficiency as you strive for another exists there, too. For example, if you care most about making life easy for users of your program, you may provide a carefully thought-out interface to it, whereas if you care most about making your own life easy, you may just do whatever is quickest for you. Neither of these is always right: it depends on the circumstances.

What the section did not discuss, but perhaps should have done, was *Pareto efficiency*. If you have a choice of two approaches in mind, and one of the approaches is more efficient in one of the ways you care about *without being less efficient in any of them*, it's a no-brainer to pick that approach.

The special thing about *maintainer efficiency* is that it is a prerequisite to improving your program in any other way.

Tip

As a beginning programmer you will seldom have to worry about the time and space efficiency of code you write. It's almost always better to focus on giving your program clear, readable structure.

If you are writing code that will operate on a lot of data, or execute a large number of times, then you may need to worry about your choice of algorithm. However, programmers worrying too much about efficiency is a more common problem than programmers worrying too little about it. In everyday cases, standard libraries, optimising compilers and intelligent run-time infrastructure will usually do a better job than you will of optimising your program for speed or space use. The difference between a million executions of a five-line loop and a thousand executions of it is *usually* not important.

So, get your program correct and clear first. Only worry about efficiency when you know you have a problem with it – your code does not run fast enough, or it uses too much space.

Then ask yourself:

* Are you using the most appropriate components from a standard library?
* Is your program doing unnecessary work?
* (For time efficiency) Is it repeating work whose results it should save the first time, and look up later?
* (For space efficiency) Is it saving work to look up later, when it would be better just to redo the work if it's needed again?

There may be particular things that, even as a beginner, you need to be aware of in your programming language: for example, if you are programming in Haskell, you will need to pay attention to whether you use `foldl` or `foldr`, and in Java, you may soon learn to build large strings using `StringBuilder` instead of just

`String`. Such things are part of learning to write idiomatic code in your language.

To go further you need some understanding of *computational complexity*. That's beyond the scope of this book. Here let us just say: some tasks, like sorting collections, have been the subject of exhaustive study and it is very well known how to write code to do them efficiently. Rather than writing your own code to carry out such a task, you should use code from an appropriate library, which is likely to be much more efficient than what you will write yourself (and will already be correct, as well). Unless you are doing an exercise where the point is to implement a sorting algorithm, don't implement your own sorting algorithm. Similarly, if your code uses data structures like dictionaries or hash tables, don't write your own, unless that's the focus of what you're doing. It's well worth spending some time becoming familiar with what is in the standard libraries available to you, so that you understand which components to use when.

Coding interviews

Curiously, a tradition has emerged that major tech companies' recruitment procedures involve asking candidates to solve small computer programming problems in highly constrained situations, such as writing the code on a white board. The problems have to be able to be stated and solved succinctly, without a lot of explanation of customer requirements, so they tend to focus on data structures and algorithms. What distinguishes a good solution from a mediocre one tends to be the time and space needed. Thus, even though, if you get the job, it may turn out to be rare for you to have to worry about such things, they may be important for getting the job. Pay close attention when you take an algorithms class, and if you are preparing for such an interview, consider a specialist book such as Gayle McDowell's *Cracking the Coding Interview*. Always write clear code, so that you can maximise the impact of your efficient code.

See this as the game that it is. You are being asked to behave like a peacock showing off its tail: the tail is not, in itself, all that important, but the mate has to choose somehow, and the tail is the chosen criterion.

10.3 Refactoring

Suppose you've realised that your program, although correct, could use some improvement. Maybe you need to remove some duplicated code, or maybe you have to replace the use of a dictionary you implemented yourself by the use of a more efficient one from a library. What do you do?

Sounds like a trick question, doesn't it? Why wouldn't you just start editing your program, and stop when you've changed it?

The reason to be careful is that you have already debugged your program, and you don't want to have to do so again. To keep your stress levels low, you want to go from a working program to a better-designed working program, without spending too much time with a non-working program in between. Refactoring – "improving the design of existing code" (Fowler, 1999) – helps you do this.

To begin with, you need a method for establishing confidence that the program is correct, which you can carry out now, and repeat on future versions of the program, as needed. That is, you need to be able to test your program, as discussed in Chapter 7.

Tip

Even if you are impatient to go on and improve your program, it really is worthwhile to take the time to make sure you have a good set of tests.

Next, your aim is to change your program in steps that are as small as you can manage, testing after each step. It's a bit like the

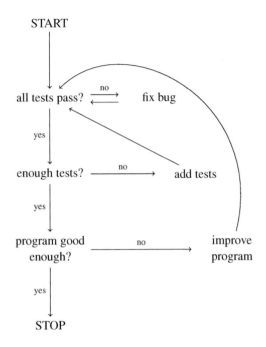

Figure 10.1. The refactoring process.

game you may have played as a child where you have to change one word into another word by changing one letter at a time, making a real word after every change. Figure 10.1 illustrates the process.

This way of working is great for keeping your stress levels low: you can arrange that you always know what you're doing and never make a change that breaks your program. It's especially useful if you are not sure how much time you will be able to spend working on the program, because every few minutes, your program returns to a fully working state, so you can stop whenever you need to.

How large your improvement steps should be is something you will learn through experience. You should usually find that all your tests pass first time, after each improvement step. If you slip into expecting that some test will fail, perhaps you might find it more efficient overall to take smaller steps. Considering our Python shopping example, some people would go all the way between our initial two versions in one go. Others might include an intermediate step, perhaps something like this:

Python example (mid refactoring)

```python
def total(basket, country):
    total = 0
    for item in basket:
        total += price(item)
    if total > 10: #free shipping offer
        return total
    else:
        total += shipping_cost(basket, country)
        return total

def shipping_cost(basket, country):
    if country == "UK" and weight(basket) <= 1:
        return STANDARD_UK_SHIPPING
    else:
        raise NotImplementedError
```

Notice that we not only run the existing set of tests after each improvement, but also ask ourselves whether there are enough tests, each time. You might decide to add specific tests for the new shipping_cost function, for example – although, if you are following a test-driven development approach (as discussed in Chapter 7), you will already have written them, before you wrote the function itself, as part of the "improve program" step.

Ideally, each refactoring step makes the program better, so that whenever you stop, the program is the best that it has been so far.

This is not always possible, however. Sometimes you find that your program needs to be restructured, and that doing the restructuring in small, refactoring steps will take you through states where the program is less clear than it is now. It is then tempting to abandon the refactoring discipline and make all your changes at once, as fast as possible. But even here, refactoring will help you to avoid getting into a buggy mess. What you should do is to make sure you understand where you are going before you start, and avoid starting until you have a suitable chunk of time available to you, so that you can take the program all the way through to its better structure without having to leave it in a working, but unsatisfactory, state. You may like to write yourself design notes or draw a picture to explain the final state you are heading for, to minimise the risk of losing your way once you start editing the code.[2]

When is the program good enough?

It really depends on the context. It is very satisfying to take a piece of code all the way to your idea of perfection, and the more often you mindfully do that, the better you will get at writing code which is good the first time. However, you will not have time to take every piece of code you ever write to perfection. More interestingly, what "perfect" is depends on what you need to do with the code: however you structure your code, some changes to the functionality will be easier to make than others. *The perfect structuring is the one that best supports the change that actually turns out to be required* – which, in real life, you can't predict with certainty! As a matter of pride, try to leave your code clean, readable, and in a state to support changes you can reasonably foresee: but don't agonise over it.

---

2 If you are fluent in Java, you might like to read Chapter 14 of *Clean Code*, which goes through an example of such a refactoring. The chapter is more than 50 pages long, though, which is why there is no such example here!

10.4 Improving Your Skills

Stretching the title of this chapter a little, what – beyond "absorb everything this book says"! – can you do to improve your skills, and hence improve *all* your programs? Let us look at one specific habit that you might find worth adopting. It is the use of katas.

> **Terminology: Kata**
>
> A kata is an exercise, performed repeatedly in order to improve one's skills.

The term originates in martial arts; Dave Thomas first introduced the idea of katas as programming exercises in *The Pragmatic Programmer*, and the idea has been taken up by others since. Other martial arts terms have also been imported into the world of programming: if you find there is a coding dojo near you, you might like to go there to do your katas.

If you are on a programming course, you may feel you have enough exercises to be going on with: why would you want more? The key is the word *repeatedly*. Instead of just doing a succession of different exercises, you adopt one and do it frequently. Fizz Buzz, which we considered in Chapter 3 and earlier in this chapter, is suitable. As you repeat an exercise you have done before, you focus on writing the program perfectly, thinking about each small choice you make along the way. You eliminate the stressful feeling that you need to get to the end in any way possible. Just as the movements of your body become second nature if you do the same physical exercise repeatedly, the elements of programming your kata should soon feel very familiar. Even though you know how to solve the problem, you don't take shortcuts: for example, you should still write tests for the program and use them as you work. Indeed, the use of katas goes well with test-driven development, and one of the things you might like to explore is how some ways of solving your problem are easier to test as you go along than others.

Tip

Even if doing daily katas doesn't sound like your kind of thing, you might want to redo an old exercise occasionally. Consider:

* getting out a solution you wrote before, and improving it in some way; or
* redoing the exercise *without* looking at your old solution, and then comparing your new solution with the old one. Did you find the exercise easier this time, or solve it better in some way? Or, perhaps, is there something you need to remind yourself of, from earlier in the course?

You can also use your katas as a basis for variation, modifying the exercise or the rules you set yourself about how to solve it. If you usually use a loop in your kata, can you write a version with recursion? Suppose you needed to add some flexibility, e.g. to vary the rules for when to print Fizz and when Buzz? If you start to use a new tool such as an IDE, programming your kata in it will help you to get used to the tool. When you start to learn a new programming language, programming your existing katas in the new language will be a useful next step after writing a Hello World program, supporting your developing understanding of the similarities and differences between the languages.

Laziness, impatience and hubris?

Another of the jokes with a serious point behind them that Larry Wall, the designer of Perl, is known for is this: he wanted to encourage programmers to develop the three most important qualities of a great programmer, viz. laziness, impatience and hubris. How could these possibly be good things to aim for, as you improve your program?

Laziness I once had a mathematics teacher who used to say "Mathematics is the art of being lazy", because so much of mathematics is about finding easy ways to do things that would be hard if you did them the obvious way. It's a similar idea: a great programmer thinks about how they can spare themselves work in future, and so writes the program in a way which will be as easy to change as possible. Even better, the great programmer makes full use of high-quality libraries: if someone else has already written the code you would have to write, you may save the effort of writing the program at all.

Impatience is the necessary counterweight to laziness. It is the quality that drives you to improve the efficiency of your program, for any kind of efficiency that's relevant to you at present. It is, for example, the quality that forces you to investigate when your program runs for longer than it reasonably should take (time efficiency). It is also the quality that tells you it is intolerable to have to change your code in five places for what is really only one reason, so that you had better improve its design so that you never have to do that again (maintainer efficiency).

Hubris means excessive pride. This is the quality that makes you want to write programs so good that everyone will admire them, and gives you confidence that you can.

At the time of writing, there is a video on YouTube entitled "Hobbits Would Make Great Programmers" in which Larry Wall explains that programmers should have the characteristics he attributes to hobbits:

- lazy in a very industrious way;
- impatient in a very patient way;
- proud in a very humble way.

11

How to Get Help (without Cheating)

What do you do when you're totally confused or stuck? Your program doesn't work, and you don't understand why, or you don't understand even how to start your next exercise. What now?

The first rule is

Don't Panic!

I apologise if that, or anything else in this chapter, seems patronising; but the fact is, many students in this situation *do* panic. They may give up, failing to submit coursework or going into exams knowing that they will fail, or dropping out of their courses. Some may cheat: they may copy someone else's answers, or even get someone else to do the work for them.

Here's what to do instead. First, identify what kind of problem you have.

1. Have you been struggling for weeks, maybe getting by with a lot of help from friends, or by looking at model answers, but have you now hit a wall?
2. Or are you generally doing fine, but feeling confused at the moment?

For example, are you confident that you completely understand the last program you wrote, and that you could write it again from scratch without help? If yes, you are likely to be in the second situation; if no, you may be in the first.

> **Tip**
>
> The learning skills you will practise as you sort yourself out are very important ones. They are more important than any individual programming skill, and will help you learn the next programming skill more easily and with less stress. So don't see the time you spend on sorting yourself out as wasted – it may be the best time you spend.

Let's discuss how to tackle the more serious situation first.

11.1 Solving a General Problem

If you are out of your depth and it's not just the current programming exercise you can't do, but the previous one and maybe the one before that, you need to take radical action. Look back through the exercises you've been set, or the exercises in your textbook, going backwards in time towards when you began learning the language. Stop when you find a collection of exercises that you're *sure* you're *completely* confident about, or at the beginning if that never happens (in that case, take the very first set of exercises in what follows). If in doubt, start at the easier set.

> **Programming exercises**
>
> You need a graded sequence of programming exercises, because you cannot learn to program without programming. You are probably given one as part of your course, but if not, find a textbook or an online course for your language that includes exercises.

("But I don't have time for this! My coursework is due in [time]!" Yes, you do. This process will get you unstuck. If you're in a significant mess, you can't submit your coursework honestly without doing something like this, and submitting it dishonestly will land you in worse trouble. Bear with me.)

Now, *without looking at any previous answer you or anyone else created*, do an exercise from this set. Next you need to check your answer. If you have tests available, or an automatic marker, run them, and be satisfied only if they show no problems. Otherwise, look at a model answer if you have one: but *first*, search your innermost being for the answer to this question:

Do you completely understand every line you wrote?

and proceed only after you've answered that question with "yes". The reasoning is that if you honestly answer "yes", then you should be in good shape to understand any respect in which the model answer differs from your answer, and see whether yours is equally correct or not.

If – which is quite likely – you find that you have some uncertainty even at this level where you thought you were completely confident, congratulate yourself on having discovered that. Make a mental note that sometimes your brain fools you into thinking you thoroughly understand something, when you don't (this is normal). Go back as far as you need to.

Right, now you're either right back at the start, or you're at a point where you *know* you can do the work up to the point where you are. Now you go forwards, but you need to try not to skip over things you don't understand, or you'll be no better off. The level of risk you undertake may depend on your circumstances, though.

Catching up properly If you can possibly find the time, go forward from here with the mindset that, this time, you're going to understand *everything* fully. Take the next chunk of your course, after the bit you definitely get. Maybe that's the next week, or the next chapter. Reread your notes, watch any relevant videos, read relevant sections of the textbook. As you do this, make a list of points you don't yet fully understand. Follow them up, if necessary using the techniques in Section 11.2 below. Once you feel confident, tackle one or two problems from the next set of exercises. You do not necessarily need to redo every exercise from every set, but you do need to get to the point where you feel confident that you could. Perhaps you might choose which exercises to tackle randomly, in order to avoid subconsciously avoiding the hard ones. Keep going forward on a solid base. This is a great thing to do with a peer: you might try pair programming your way through some past exercises, taking it in turns to be the one at the keyboard.

Terminology: Pair programming

Pair programming is when two people program together at one computer. One of them is in charge of the actual typing, while the other acts as lookout: is the program going in the right direction, and are there any rocks ahead? That is, is the person typing following a strategy that will lead to a good program, and are there any problems or bugs?

Pair programming is a practice which is sometimes used by professional programmers (especially in agile development), because, even though it takes more time, it can lead to higher-quality programs. As a student, you may find it a good way to learn.

Skimming If you're really, really pushed for time, you can try taking a shortcut like this, but be aware that it has risks and may backfire. Go forward identifying the *key points* of the material, and checking that you understand them, but being prepared to skip over things that don't seem relevant to the exercise you're stuck on. For example, if you find a section of your notes that's about how to read from standard input, and your exercise doesn't require doing that, you could skip that section for now. Do, however, make a note to remind yourself to go back to it later.

Compared with catching up properly, skimming can save you time, but the risk is that you may not be reliable at identifying what's relevant – later material tends to depend on earlier material in ways that aren't always completely obvious.

11.2 Solving a More Specific Problem

If you have been doing fine, but are feeling confused right now, then handling the situation well is the key to ensuring that you do not end up with a more general problem in future.

The first step is to analyse what it is that's confusing. If your problem is a compile-time or run-time error, or a particular case where your program gives surprising results, the techniques discussed in Chapter 9 are probably what you want. If you have a program that works properly sometimes, but not always, then systematically testing it, as described in Chapter 7, is the next step.

11.2.1 Getting Help from and with Error Messages

What if your problem is that you *keep* getting a particular kind of error message, suggesting that there's something about the language that you systematically don't understand? In Chapter 9 we briefly mentioned that one of the most useful things you can do with an error message you don't understand is, surprisingly perhaps, paste it into your favourite search engine. This works better the more popular your language is, but if you're lucky, it will take you straight to one or more pages where some helpful people explain exactly what it means and how to fix the problems that give rise to it. However, there are some reasons to be wary.

- Don't go too far down a rabbit hole. Some error messages arise in a wide variety of circumstances, and it's easy to get sucked into trying to understand a discussion about why someone *else* gets a certain error message, while *you* get it for a different reason.
- Be careful with solutions you do not fully understand. If you paste someone else's code into your program, you can make matters worse. It can be useful to see whether or not a possible solution works in your context or not, but always delimit code you got from elsewhere clearly in your program with comments. If you are submitting code for assessment, this may well be required anyway.

• If you will be being assessed in a situation where you won't have access to the internet, beware of getting too dependent on this, or any other search-based, technique.

The other thing you can do is try to analyse *why* you don't understand the message. One of the reasons why error messages are so often hard to understand is that they are written tersely, using terminology that experts in the language understand but that beginners do not. If you can identify a piece of terminology you're not understanding, then looking it up (in the language documentation, or in your favourite search engine again) may well help.

For example, here's an error message of a kind that C compilers sometimes produce:

> foo.c:8: error: lvalue required as left operand of assignment

It makes perfect sense and is likely to be very helpful – *provided* that you know what the terms "lvalue", "operand" and "assignment" mean in C.

11.2.2 Finding Explanations and Helpful Code

Sometimes as you struggle with a problem it may occur to you that you cannot possibly be the first person to encounter it. A search may be fruitful, but the caveats mentioned when we discussed searching for error messages apply here too. The more generic the thing you want to do, and the more widely used your language, the more likely it is that searching will help. For example, searching

 java read from file

yields good explanations of something that is notorious for tripping up newcomers to Java.

When you do such a search, you may well come across a piece of code that appears, from the context – perhaps a tutorial or an answer to a question on a forum – to be likely to be useful to you. Copy-pasting such code is usually unwise even if it is permitted. It is better to read it carefully to enhance your own understanding, then put it aside and use your new understanding to write your own code. This reduces the risk that you copy-paste code that you do not really understand, and hence end up with a program that you do not understand: this is a liability. If you do copy-paste, or if you are in any doubt about whether you have completely understood what you found, always add comments to indicate where you found the suggestion you are following, and what code you got from where; you might want to go back and read some accompanying explanation again in future.

> **Tip**
>
> Look out for dates on material you find online and be alert to the possibility that it is written for an old version of your language.

Using standard libraries is the safest way to make use of code you did not write. If the functionality you want is in such a library, you should always avoid writing your own version of it (unless that is the specific point of an exercise you are doing). Spend some time browsing the documentation of the standard library, if your language has one: good use of it can save you vast amounts of effort.

Using a non-standard library – that is, a library of code that you can import into your program and make use of, but that is not automatically available to anyone using your language – is an interesting intermediate case, especially when you find you have a choice of either doing that or writing (or copying) your own code to do what the library could do for you. The advantage of using the library is separation of concerns: your code can stay focused on its main task, while the library provides functionality you simply use. The disadvantage is that your code now has a new *dependency* on the library. Someone who does not have access to the library will not be able to use your code, and if the library disappears or breaks in future, you will have a problem.

11.2.3 Getting Help with a Complex Program

Suppose you have got to a stage where your program is too complex to expect anyone else to read, but you are totally stuck: there is something about its behaviour that you do not understand, and your attempts at debugging have failed so badly that you have no real idea what you ought to be improving about the program. In an ideal world, this is a "don't start from here" situation: you aim to keep your program clear, well-structured and completely understood, at all times. However, back in the real world, it sometimes happens – indeed, even if you yourself have impeccable habits, sometimes you may run into such a problem when you have to work with code you did not write.

Do not dismiss the possibility of starting again. If you have a few hundred lines of code, or less, and you realise that it is a nasty mess of spaghetti code, it may be quickest to start with a blank file, this time keeping the code clear, ensuring that you understand every line of it, and carefully testing as you go.

Starting again is not always the right answer, however; sometimes it is impractical, and sometimes it simply seems unnecessary: perhaps your code seems fairly clear, except that something is not working as you expect and you cannot sort out why clearly enough to get rid of the problem. Well: if you can't get rid of the problem directly, you need to get rid of the complexity, leaving the problem in place, to enable someone to help you.

Making a minimal non-working example It might seem odd to deliberately construct a new program that doesn't work. But having a small, simple program that doesn't work *in the same way as a program you care about* turns out to be useful.

> ### Terminology: Minimal non-working example
>
> A minimal non-working example (MNWE) – for a particular problem – is the smallest, simplest program you can construct that still has the problem.

A small, simple program is easier for you to understand, so there's a good chance that once you look carefully at it, you'll be able to work out what's wrong. Having a MNWE is even more important if you ask someone else for help – the less they have to read that's not relevant to the problem, the more quickly and easily they can understand what's going on and help you, and the more likely it is that they will be willing to do so.

To build it, take a copy of your program that contains a problem, and start cutting and commenting parts out. Each time you make a change, do whatever you need to do – e.g. recompile, rerun – to check that the problem is still there. Concretely, I suggest starting with the part of the program that you are *most* confident is not relevant to the problem. Comment it out, replacing it with a dummy if necessary. For example, if you are commenting out the body of a piece of code that should return an integer, and you believe it doesn't matter (for your problem) what integer it returns, you might comment out the actual calculation and put in a statement returning 0 instead. Reprocess the program and check that, as expected, the problem still occurs. Having checked that, delete the commented out code. This helps to make the code you're looking at get visually simpler, which in turn makes it more likely that you'll understand what's going on.

It may happen that at some point, you remove some code you expected to be irrelevant, and to your surprise, the problem vanishes or changes. Such a surprise may well help you progress towards understanding – but this is why you should check frequently that you have not inadvertently made the problem go away.

What usually happens is that somewhere in the process of making your MNWE, you come to understand what's going on. Sometimes this understanding arrives like a thunderbolt. Other times, it's more that once your example gets really simple, you can see that the problem *must* lie with some particular language or library feature. Then you read the documentation of that feature carefully, and learn how to fix your own problem.

If that doesn't happen, though, and you keep on simplifying the program until any further simplification makes the problem disappear, you are still a lot further on than you were, because now you have a small program whose behaviour you don't understand in quite a simple way, and you can take it to someone who might be able to help. As it's now a long way away from an actual answer to a coursework question, you'll probably feel comfortable sharing it with a fellow student who might understand it better than you do (check local policies, though!). Alternatively, if you take it to an instructor, they are likely to be able to give you help quickly and easily, because your example is no longer cluttered with things that are irrelevant to your problem.

11.2.4 Asking for Help

More generally, when should you ask for help, and from whom? If you're stuck on a specific exercise that will be assessed, you may first need to check what kind of help or discussion with others is permitted. Most likely, if the exercise is formative (usually: not for credit) some level of discussion with your peers will be allowed, but if it is summative (for credit) you'll usually be expected to do it entirely alone.

If you are allowed to discuss it with peers, this can be very constructive. However, it can also lead you to think you understand more than you do, so be careful. There's a big gap, in practice, between being able to understand when someone else tells you how to solve a problem, and being able to come up with the solution for yourself. So don't get too dependent on help from others, and look for opportunities to give help as well as take it.

Many courses offer some kind of course forum, where students are encouraged to ask for help. This has advantages and disadvantages compared with talking directly to another human being. On the plus side, your question is likely to reach more people, more quickly, than you can talk to face to face – so the chance is higher that one of them will be able and willing to help. Less obviously, the process of turning your problem into a clear, succinct textual question often helps you clarify your thinking. It's not at all uncommon to find that, in the process of working out how to ask your question, you answer it for yourself. (This is a similar phenomenon to the cardboard debugging process that we discussed in Chapter 9.) On the minus side, you have to take the time to do the writing – which will be harder, the more confused you are – and you may have to wait for a response.

> **Tip**
>
> Even when you are writing only for people on the same course as you, write carefully, and give relevant detail. For example, don't just say "it doesn't work" or "it gives an error" – say exactly how it doesn't work, or exactly what error you see.

Should you turn to the wider internet? There are sites like StackOverflow[1] that are set up for programmers to ask questions about programming. I'd urge you to be cautious about this, as an early-stage student. It's likely that your question can be sorted out by reading standard documentation, or has been asked before, and the denizens of StackOverflow can be impatient with such questions.

---

1 https://stackoverflow.com

However, "be cautious" doesn't mean never do it: it just means take care to be asking a question which is as clear and precise as possible. Don't ask "why doesn't this work?", for example; say "I expect this code to return 4 on input 1, but instead it returns 3 – why?" Say what standard resources you have consulted and why closely related questions don't answer yours. Do include an example of the code feature you're talking about – perhaps an example of code whose behaviour you don't fully understand, or an example of code you think should work but doesn't – but make sure this piece of code is a true MNWE (see above), so that experts can understand as quickly as possible what the essential point you're stuck on is.

For a lot more discussion of what constitutes a well-asked question, I recommend you read the most famous Smart Questions guide, "How to ask questions the smart way" (Raymond, 2014).

Finally, a trivial point that seems to get overlooked:

> **Tip**
>
> Any time you send someone your code, post it on a forum, etc., copy in your actual program text, rather than including an image of it! Most people, in helping you, will want to try out your code, or their modified version of it, in their own tool: you need to allow them to copy and paste, not retype.

11.2.5 Help to Get Started

What if it's not that you have a problem with a program you have written, but rather that you have no idea how to even get started, so that when you think about asking someone else, you can't really even work out what question to ask? This tends to be a problem that afflicts beginners, which experienced programmers often have trouble helping with, because they have long forgotten ever feeling that way. The positive way to think about this is that, one day, this feeling will be a distant memory for you too.

In the meantime, what can you do? Perhaps you'd like to reread Chapter 3, especially Section 3.5. But maybe you feel as though you were fine with small problems, but now you're facing a more challenging task and you don't know how to get started with that?

One thing is to polish off any easy bits: reduce the part you can't do to something as small as possible.

Tip

"When faced with a problem you do not understand, do any part of it you do understand, then look at it again."

Robert A. Heinlein (Heinlein, 1966)

A related technique is to see if you can invent a simpler, easier version of the problem and solve that to begin with, as a way in.

11.3 How to Cope When Your Teacher Is Confusing You

Finally, a word about how to deal with a situation where you are confused even without a programming problem in front of you. What should you do when you come out of a lecture, say, feeling you understand less than you did when you went in?

As always, the first instruction is not to panic. It is *not* a sign that you can't do programming and should give up now. People who teach programming are attempting to help you – but sometimes we don't succeed. However, it is a sign that you should take some kind of action. Here, as in other cases, the right action will depend on how general your confusion is.

The commonest explanation is that there is something the teacher was assuming that you already understood, which in fact you have not absorbed. Can you tell what that is likely to be? It may be obvious: for example, perhaps you missed last week's sessions through illness, and need to make a plan to catch up. Similarly, if you are behind with doing some exercises, that may be the explanation: to learn programming, you must program, so you can't leave the exercises until later.

Perhaps, though, the teacher is accidentally assuming everyone knows something that has not been taught. The first thing to do is to ask around: are other people confused about the same thing? Either way you win: if you find someone who is not confused, they can probably help you; if you find someone who is confused, you are no longer alone.

> **Tip**
>
> Do not suffer in silence. If, after trying the obvious things, you are still confused, ask your teacher!

People differ in how they learn, so it is worth spending some time gathering resources that suit you. Perhaps there is a recommended text you should get; or you might find it useful to go to a library or bookshop and browse until you find something that appeals to you. Or try searching online for tutorial material. YouTube is a great source of explanatory snippets, too. For example, if you were confused by a lecture on Haskell's list comprehension, you can search for that and find many videos attempting to explain it. You might try a few – if one doesn't seem clear, just try the next. Once you find a good video, it's worth seeing if it comes from a channel you might want to subscribe to.

Usually, it's a good idea to use these other resources *in addition to* continuing to follow your course as you're expected to. For example, go to all the lectures even if you don't always understand them (and even if they are recorded). At the very least, this will help you to stay in touch with roughly what is being covered – and you may find you get better at following them with practice.

12

How to Score Well in Coursework

This chapter focuses on what we might call the mark-mercenary aspects of being a student. Its principal aim is not to make you a better programmer, as such. It's to help you maximise the number of marks you get on a coursework assignment, wherever your programming skills are at the time. However, there is one way in which it may help you grow as a programmer. If you make sure that you get as many marks as your current programming skills will let you get, any places where you *do* lose marks should correspond to things that you genuinely don't fully understand yet. That means that the feedback you get should be well targeted: you won't just read it and think "oh yes, I know that", but instead, you will be able to learn from it. Moreover, I notice that, as an educator, I have been unable to prevent some of this chapter slipping into "how to learn as much as possible from coursework".

12.1 Seven Golden Rules

1. Start early. Most things take longer than you think, and there may well be "waiting" time involved, e.g. where you discover one evening that you need to talk to an instructor who won't be available until the following afternoon.

   Students often wonder whether they can start their assignment early – "do we have all the material yet?" The simplest way to deal with that is to ask. Keeping well up with the course material will also help, as it will help you to be sure that, when you encounter something that doesn't look familiar, you definitely haven't met it yet.

Remember that you can be proactive and look things up even if they haven't come up in class yet, and that's often a useful thing to do.

"Pulling an all-nighter" near the deadline has its attractions, especially if you can do so in a lab full of other people doing the same; it can lead to a feeling of camaraderie and even of euphoria once you finally complete the exercise. But it really, truly isn't a good way to optimise either your mark or your learning. When you are very tired, you make mistakes, and you also fail to store things you learn in long-term memory.

2. Read the question. I know, I know, you've been told this before. In programming assignments, it has several aspects. There are book-keeping things like ensuring that you know whether, when and how you must hand the work in, and whether there are rules about things like what your files must be called. Those things apply to any kind of coursework, not only programming assignments. On the other hand, in a programming assignment, the details, of what your program must do, assume huge importance. You can't just read the description the way you're reading this book: you will need to look at it word by word, and make sure you follow the instructions *precisely*.

3. Follow all the advice in Chapter 7, to test your work and make sure you've done it right.

4. If you encounter something you don't understand, in the sense that you think the question you are being asked is ambiguous or vague, make the issue concrete by programming it in two ways. Sometimes, as you try to do this, you will find that in reality only one of the two ways makes sense. If that happens, you have solved your own problem. If you do end up with two interpretations that seem equally plausible, you can ask your instructor which way is what they want. For an instructor, a question of the form "do you want X, or Y?" is easier to understand and answer clearly than a question like "what does this mean?"

5. Follow all the advice in Chapter 8, so that you get any part marks that may be going. This applies especially if a large part of your mark will come not from automated tests, but from a human reading your code. Any human doing that is likely to be busy and tired, and anything you can do to make it easier for them to see what's right about your answer is likely to help you maximise your mark.

6. Don't cheat! Even if you get away with it this time – and you may not – you'll harm your learning and put yourself in a worse position going forward.

7. Do hand the work in on time.

12.2 Lab Exercises

What I mean by "lab exercises" here is: relatively small, straightforward programming exercises intended to help an individual learn a programming language. Typically a lab exercise does not invite much creativity: what you have to do is tightly specified, and is straightforward once you are familiar with the language. A first programming course often includes a sequence of such exercises, covering whatever features of the language are included in the course. They may be marked for credit or not, and model solutions may or may not be available.

We start with these because of their special character: they are so valuable to your learning that doing them will help maximise your marks on whatever other assessment there is, even if they don't attract credit in themselves.

> **Tip**
>
> If you don't have a sequence of exercises like this that you must do, find one. For example, choose a textbook for your language which includes many small exercises, and do them.

The reason is simple: you cannot learn to program by reading about it, watching someone else do it, or any means at all other than actually doing it. That's not to say that other modalities aren't important, of course, but they are additional to programming, not alternatives.

Beyond following the Seven Golden Rules, how can you maximise your marks on such exercises, if there are marks, while at the same time maximising the benefit you get from them?

The main thing I advise is to think of your progress with each exercise in levels, as follows:

1. I've read the question and started to think about the exercise.
2. I've written some code.
3. It does the right thing in some cases.
4. It does the right thing in all cases, as far as I can tell.
5. I thoroughly understand every line of my code.
6. As far as I can tell, my code is perfect.

You don't have to reach level 6 for every exercise, but the further up you get, the more you will learn. Keep a record, for each exercise, of which level you have reached.

Level 5 needs a word of explanation. It's normal that as you learn the language, there are features you don't fully understand, so that you try things out, which sometimes work as you expect, and sometimes don't. When something works, it's natural to breathe a sigh of relief and go on to the next issue. Even better, though, is to be sure you know why it works, and what the effect would be of changing each small part, so that you could confidently explain it to someone else. To get to that level, you'll probably need to use a combination of reading reference material for your language and experimentation.

12.3 Individual Projects

An individual project is a piece of coursework that affords you more opportunity for creativity: you have considerable choice about what your software does and how.

To maximise your marks, first find out everything you can about how marks will be allocated and what the criteria are. For example, do you have to write a report, do a demonstration, submit the code? Are you allowed or encouraged to find and build on other software, or not? Are you supposed to be demonstrating particular skills or kinds of learning?

Once you have whatever information is available, you may well find yourself disappointed that there isn't much. The more flexibility there is in the task, the more difficulty instructors will have in giving marks objectively. Paradoxically, in that case you will usually maximise your mark – and certainly get the most benefit – if you worry about marks as little as you can. Approach the project in a way that interests you, and try to get engrossed in it. I recommend estimating how much time you should spend, and then tracking the time you do spend, explicitly. This is because open-ended, long-term tasks can be hard to balance against smaller exercises with tight deadlines. It is common for students – and others! – to find that, somehow, the task without a looming deadline never gets a look-in. Finally, avoid spending a lot of time on things that are not really programming – designing graphic art for an app, for example – unless you enjoy it enough to be able to count that time as recreation, or have personal reasons for wanting to learn skills outside those that are being examined.

12.4 Team Working

Working in teams is a common part of programming coursework, and it comes in many flavours. You may be assigned to a team, or allowed to group yourselves into teams; you may self-organise or be managed by someone else; you may or may not have to reflect on the experience.

My main advice here is to take the whole exercise with a large grain of salt: working in a group with other students is almost nothing like working with a team of colleagues in a real software development situation. In particular, you may hate the former and nevertheless love the latter, so don't worry if you hate the coursework team experience!

The key to maximising your marks is to understand how marks will be allocated. Does everyone's mark depend only on the quality of the jointly developed software, or is there some mechanism intended to enforce that every team member contributes? Sometimes you may be asked to estimate how much effort each team member has put in, and the estimates may affect the distribution of marks, for example.

Student teams often find themselves with one or two members who are so much stronger (either in skills or in dedication) than the rest that the way to maximise the quality of the software that gets written is to allow them to carry the rest of the team, writing or rewriting all or most of the software. This situation is difficult for everyone to handle. If you are one of the strong team members, you will need to decide how far you are willing to do more than your "fair share". If you can truthfully say that it won't help your teammates' scores for you to do the work for them, so much the better. If you are one of the weaker team members in this situation, it is important to remember the long view: you don't *only* want a good mark for this exercise, you also want to improve your own skills. So make sure you get to do a decent amount of the programming, even if you have a team member who could do it faster.

For everyone's benefit, the team should try to ensure that members teach one another how to solve problems, rather than just solving them. This helps the members being taught at any moment, but it may help the team members doing the teaching even more. The saying "the best way to learn something is to teach it" is a cliché for a reason: it's absolutely true. More generally, friendly and cooperative interactions within the team help you to improve your interpersonal skills, which will be part of the point of the exercise.

12.5 Demonstrations

You may be expected to demonstrate your code working, and discuss it with someone, as part of the process. This can be fun, especially if you made some decisions that you are proud of: you'll get a chance to draw attention to things that, otherwise, a marker might simply overlook. It may also give you a good opportunity to mention anything you want specific feedback on.

It can be difficult to convince yourself that it's necessary to spend time preparing for a demonstration, if there isn't a piece of written work to produce. For a smooth experience, do check the following:

1. When and where is your demonstration?
2. Who needs to be there? E.g. in the case of a team project, everyone on the team, or just one person to demonstrate?
3. What have you been told about the timing and format? E.g. if you have to pre-plan a demonstration, how long must it be and what must it cover?
4. Will you use a computer and software environment identical to what you've been used to? If there are any differences at all, do practise beforehand on the demonstration environment, if you possibly can – it's easy to be tripped up by details, such as not having your usual IDE available.
5. If you will have to connect a laptop to a data projector, do you know how to do this successfully – for example, if you need a special adapter, do you have one?
6. Is the demonstration itself (as opposed to the program you are demonstrating) assessed, and if so, what do you know about the criteria?

Be aware that part of the reason for asking a student to demonstrate their code working is to gain confidence that the student genuinely wrote the code: the underlying assumption is that someone will be able to explain how the code works if (and only if) they wrote it. This is debatable – but in any case, being sure you understand how your code works is a good thing!

Practising the demonstration beforehand to someone else, such as a fellow student, is a very good idea; many people find it quite nerve-racking to demonstrate, and practice is the best way to calm nerves. As you practise you are likely to find small things you want to improve; for example, if you try explaining your code to someone else, you may well notice ways in which it is not as clearly written as it could be.

Tip

Never assume that some last-minute change you made "couldn't possibly make any difference". If you change *anything* about your program, run through the demonstration again to check that everything still works as you expect.

12.6 Reflective Writing

You may be surprised if you are asked to write about your experience doing a programming exercise, but this happens quite often. As for demonstrations, one reason for it is that the people running the course are worried about whether you really wrote the code you submitted. They think that by getting you to write about the experience, they reduce the risk that you just copied the code, or bought it. Less cynically, such writing exercises also aim to help you consolidate what you have learned from the programming, by reflecting on it and making any lessons explicit.

Of course you have to follow any instructions you're given about what to include. Typically, though, a marker will be looking for at least these three things.

- Some content that is sufficiently specific that it goes with your code and not with someone else's. So, mention your code's structural elements by name, and explain why you structured your code that way.
- Some evidence that you learned something, and that you know what that is. So, say what you learned! For example, describe a problem you had, how you solved it, and what you now understand that would help you not to have the same problem again.

- Clear writing – not only because clear writing is easier for the marker to read, but also because the ability to write clearly is a key "transferable skill" that the course as a whole is probably trying to give you. You don't need to produce a literary master-piece, but do read your work aloud, preferably to someone else, before you submit it, to check that it makes sense and you haven't missed out words (which is surprisingly easy to do). Run a spell-checker, too.

People differ in how they experience reflective writing. If you find that it genuinely helps you to fix what you have learned in your head, remember that. In that case, perhaps you would like to do a little reflective writing regularly, even when it isn't required? Some people like to keep a Learning Diary for such things. Others would rather go paddling in ice-cold treacle than do such a thing. Only you know how you feel about it!

13

How to Score Well in a Programming Exam

Like the chapter on scoring well in an assignment, this one focuses on how you can maximise your marks, given your current state of competence. It's a good chapter to reread a day or two before the exam.

A "programming exam" could mean a traditional pencil and paper exam where you have to write code on paper, or it could mean an exam where you will write a program, on a computer, under exam conditions. Personally I really dislike the former, because it feels *so* unnatural; but computerised programming exams are quite hard to organise, so you may still encounter paper-based programming exams. Stretching a point, it could even mean a multiple-choice exam that tests your knowledge of programming.

While the basic task of learning to program is the same regardless of how it will be examined, knowing what kind of assessment to expect can help you to organise your knowledge in an accessible way, to maximise your performance. Much of the preparation you will need to do is the same, regardless of the exam type, but this chapter will also have some specific pointers for each kind of exam.

13.1 Preparing for the Exam

There are two main things you need to do well in advance of the exam: find out all about what to expect, and practise. Past papers, for similar assessments at your institution, are an important tool for both. If there is a plentiful supply of past papers, use one recent paper for understanding what to expect, reserving a different one for practising.

13.1.1 Finding Out What to Expect

First – as early as you like – look at a past paper, without reading it in detail. How long is it? What *kind* of questions are being asked? What is the rubric (i.e. what choice of questions, if any, do you have)? What is the pass mark? Is there a mark, short of 100%, that you personally would be comfortable with? How much of the paper would you have to do perfectly in order to score that mark?

Next, look in more detail at the style of question being asked. Are there many short questions, or just one or two long ones? Do you have to write whole programs, or program snippets? Are there questions that ask you to use a specific programming language feature, such as recursion? Make sure, in that case, that you haven't got into the habit of "programming around" something you don't understand. In real life it's often possible to be a (fairly) productive programmer in a language while avoiding some feature you don't like, but here you're trying to maximise your mark.

What, if anything, are you allowed to take in with you? Exams vary from completely "closed book", where you can take in nothing, through intermediate situations where you might be allowed only a clean copy of a course book, to completely "open book" exams where you can take in anything you like on paper, and (for computer-based exams) perhaps even a USB stick. If you are allowed to take things in, think about what will be useful.

What are the rules concerning asking questions in the exam? Is there a mechanism for asking for clarification if you think a question is unclear? (Where I work, it is possible to ask the invigilator to contact the person who set the exam with a clarification question, but I advise students against doing this unless they really cannot proceed without more input. Especially, if other people in the room appear unconcerned, you can probably save yourself time and stress by reading the paper again with minute attention, and answering your own question!)

Finally, a meta-level question: how closely will the real paper resemble the past papers? In your institution, does the exam setter have a great deal of freedom to decide to set a different style of paper this time, or is it safe to assume that the paper you will sit will be very similar in style to the ones you have seen?

13.1.2 Practising a Past Paper

When you have, in principle, learned (almost) all of the material that will be examined, it's good to do a past paper. You probably don't have many representative papers to use (courses, and indeed programming languages, tend to change over the years) so it's important to make the best use of them. It's a waste, for example, to read all the available papers before you attempt to do one under exam conditions, because then you rob yourself of the chance to practise reading an unfamiliar paper under time pressure.

> **Tip**
>
> Even though it's scary and you may feel you know you won't do well, do a past paper under the same conditions you'll encounter in the real thing.

If you find the paper quite doable, great. If you find the paper very difficult when you do it in this way, that's great too – it gives you lots of useful information. Did you run out of time, or run out of questions you could attempt? Which parts, if any, could you do? Where did you get stuck? If you think carefully about these questions, you are well-placed to target your remaining work. In rather concrete subjects, like programming, it's common to get stuck on small points in exams, so a practice in which you identify and remove such small sticking-points can be really worthwhile.

There may or may not be model solutions and/or examiner's notes available for a past paper. These can be useful, but *on no account* look at them until you have tried the paper yourself. It is easy to fool yourself into mistaking "I can read the model solution" for "I could have written the model solution." You need to be able to write good code, not just read it!

Tip

"The first principle is that you must not fool yourself – and you are the easiest person to fool."

Richard Feynman (Feynman, 1974)

13.1.3 Planning for the Exam

If the exam is open book: plan what to take with you. (Maybe this book!) Make sure you know your way around whatever you take – this is not a good time to try using something you're not familiar with. Don't take too much; when you're nervous, you don't want to be faffing with too much paper.

Ask yourself: What will you have trouble remembering? Make a list of reminders and take it in with you, if that's allowed, or else memorise it.

Bearing in mind the information you gathered about the exam, develop a strategy about whether you should work as fast as possible to at least attempt everything on the paper, or whether it's better to work meticulously to do part of the paper perfectly, even at the expense of not finishing. Usually, the latter will be a better strategy, but not always.

13.2 In the Exam

When you first open the paper, read through it quickly to verify that nothing is dramatically different from what you expect. (If something is, and it is not because you are in the wrong room, remind yourself that everyone else is probably just as surprised as you are. There is no reason why you should not cope, given that you have become pretty skilled at writing good programs.)

As discussed in Chapter 12, it's essential to *read the questions* carefully. It may be more difficult in an exam, because you're likely to be feeling stressed, and because you probably won't have the opportunity to ask informally for clarification.

Both for paper exams and for computer exams, it will be important to write clear code – although the reasons are different in each case, and we will give them in the separate sections that follow.

13.3 Specific Points for Paper Exams

If you will be doing a programming exam on paper, make sure (ask, well in advance, if necessary) that you understand the expectations. Do you have to get the syntax perfectly correct, for example, or do you only have to write something close enough that the examiner believes you have the right idea?

See it from the examiner's, and marker's, point of view. Marking code that is written on paper is quite painful. They will be looking for something in your code that's quick to recognise – nobody wants to sit with a large pile of scripts simulating a complex program in their head! How can you make it easier for them to *see* quickly that your code is correct?

> ### Hoare's two ways to construct a software design
>
> Tony Hoare famously wrote in his paper "The Emperor's Old Clothes" that "there are two ways of constructing a software design: One way is to make it so simple that there are *obviously* no deficiencies and the other way is to make it so complicated that there are no *obvious* deficiencies." Always, but especially in a paper-based programming exam, you should use the former – more difficult – approach.

13.4 Specific Points for Computer-Based Exams

Writing code on a computer is more natural than writing it on paper, but programming exams on a computer may still have artificial constraints unlike anything you've encountered before.

Such programming exams often differ from coursework assignments in that they have to be marked very fast, and very reliably, in large numbers. They are highly likely to be marked, at least in part, by automated tests. Things you need to check include:

• What computing environment will you be in? Will you be expected to do the exam on a laptop of your own, maybe with some special software that you'll have to install? Or will you have to work on a lab machine? What tools will be available to you? How will you submit your work?
• You will probably not be allowed access to the internet: but will you be provided with any libraries or documentation?
• What are the basic marking guidelines? For example, if you submitted code that didn't compile correctly, would it get an automatic zero (because it wouldn't be possible to run the automated tests on it) or would a human marker look at it and maybe give it some marks?

In the exam, keep your code clear. You are under stress and more likely than usual to make mistakes. Don't invite those mistakes by poor indentation or badly chosen variable names. Even if your work will be marked purely by a computer, ensuring your code stays readable will help *you* to read it as you check it, debug it and try to improve it. You have time for this: provided you've practised the techniques beforehand, they won't slow you down.

Even if non-compiling code can get some marks, do make sure your code compiles without error! If you work in an IDE, make use of any information it gives you about problems in your code, too.

Test your work. If you are given tests, use those first. Use any examples in the question paper. Then, create extra examples of your own, following the hints in Chapter 7 to pick the inputs that are most likely to expose any problems. Depending on your language, the environment and your own expertise, you might write automated tests, or you might just run your program manually on the examples.

13.5 What about Multiple Choice Exams?

Since programming exams where you actually write programs are quite tricky to mark, you may find you're being examined by a multiple choice exam instead. The questions may be straightforward, examining the same kind of skills you'd use in another kind of exam. Or, they may be chosen to examine your knowledge of dark corners of the language. Don't assume that because it's multiple choice it'll be easy: it's possible to set arbitrarily difficult multiple choice exams! If you have past papers available, try one out. Find out what the exam's policy is on wrong answers – are they penalised, in which case you shouldn't guess, or not, in which case you might as well?

> **Tip**
>
> Try setting your own questions. Even better, do this with a group of friends, swap questions, and discuss the answers. You will gain insight both into what questions can be asked, and into what you do and don't understand.

14

How to Choose a Programming Language

If you're a student – or, indeed, a teacher! – you will often have no choice about what programming language to use in a course you are committed to. By now, I hope you have some techniques for getting to grips with the prescribed language, whatever it is.

What if you do have a choice of what language to use for a project, though, or a choice of what programming language to learn next? Many factors may influence your decision, from the nature of a program you want to write, to your own state of mind.

14.1 Questions to Consider

Are You Choosing Just for Yourself? Or are you writing a program with someone else, or that someone else will have to maintain in future? You may have to take other people's needs and preferences into account.

What Is the Task? Each language is better for some tasks than others. Actually, though, this isn't as big a factor as you might think. All the languages you are likely to consider are Turing complete, so you can, in principle, program anything you like in them. However, depending on the tools and libraries available, some may be more practical than others. If you can describe the general area of a relevant task (say "data analysis" or "VR game") in a few words, you might like to search

 programming language *your_task*

to get some ideas of languages to consider.

Terminology: Turing machine

In 1936, Alan Turing described a simple mathematical model of a computer, which we now call, in his honour, the *Turing machine*. The *Turing-computable functions* are the mathematical functions (the mappings from input to output) that can be expressed using such a machine. You might expect that your choice of programming language would have an important effect on which functions you could express. Remarkably, this turns out not to be so. Although programming languages differ in what can be *conveniently* expressed, modern programming languages do not have, in principle, any more expressive power than very old ones, or even than Turing machines. We call any language in which you can program all the Turing-computable functions *Turing complete*.

Which Language(s) Do You Know Already? This factor can operate either way. You may prefer to use a language you're already familiar with, even if it isn't ideal for the task, so that you can focus on things other than the nitty gritty of how you make the machine do what you want. However, it can be more fun to use a language that's new to you, and – especially early in your programming life – it may be positively sensible to take the opportunity to widen your range. Writing a program you want written is the best way to develop fluency in a language. It'll take a bit longer than if you do it in a language you already know, of course, but you may learn more in the process.

How Long Will the Program Need to Last? If it must last for many years, you may prefer to use a long-established language with a reputation for maintaining backwards compatibility, like Java, rather than a fast-moving language in which old programs often have to be changed if they are to work with the latest version of the language, like Haskell.[1] Note, though, that you don't always know how long your program will last. If it turns out to be useful, it may last much longer than you expect!

Do You Plan to Distribute It? If you want other people to be able to compile and/or run your program, you need to pay attention to how easy it will be for them. What will they need in the way of compiler, run-time software, libraries, etc., and how likely are they to have the necessary things installed already? Will you need to provide instructions? Are there other dependencies or constraints? For example, what are you assuming about what operating system these people will be using?

What Kind of Libraries or Components Will You Need? E.g. does your program need a graphical user interface (GUI), or to use a

---

1 Strictly speaking, Haskell – the official language – has been very stable; what changes often is the commonly used Glasgow Haskell Compiler.

database? Check that good, suitable software that interacts well with your language exists. For example, if you want your program to have a GUI, search

 gui *your_language*

Be quite cautious: sometimes you may find that there is a library, but that it is out of date, poorly documented, or hard to use. Unless you are really looking for a challenge, you should look for evidence that plenty of other people currently use the software you are considering.

What Kind of Mistakes Are Most Important to Guard Against? This question, and its implications, are harder to get a handle on than some of the others, but are worth thinking about. For example, if your program will manipulate complex data structures, you may find the security of static type-checking important. On the other hand, if your program will involve a frequently changing interaction at the command line and lots of file handling, it might be more important to you that your language has convenient operating system interaction and string manipulation features.

14.2 A Few Languages You May Encounter

Here is a list of just a few languages, focusing on the ones you are most likely to need to learn for university study. Perhaps you might challenge yourself to learn a little of each?

Any such list is bound to be incomplete and controversial, however. If you come across a language that interests you, do not be put off learning it by the fact that it is not included here!

C C is a low-level language, in the sense that it is "close to the machine": every computer has a C compiler. It may be a good choice if you want to understand how your program really works; for example, by learning about pointer arithmetic, you can improve your intuition for how data is stored in the computer's memory. It is still a popular language for embedded systems. If you are interested in hardware, you are very likely to need to learn it.

C++ layers object-oriented features on top of C. It is harder to write in than Java, but even today it is more efficient. If C++ is the right language for you, you probably don't need me to explain why that is.

Fortran dates back to the 1950s and is now thought of as an old-fashioned language. However, it is still widely used in scientific computing.

Haskell Haskell is one of the best established functional languages. It has a powerful static type system which can help you to avoid many kinds of bug. It is the language of choice for many experts in programming language theory. This has pluses and minuses: a plus is that learning Haskell will make many advanced features and a body of research available to you, while a minus is that it can be hard to get simple answers to simple questions, and that the compilers and libraries tend to change fast and unpredictably.

Java Java is a very widely used, robust language, well-supported by tools, books, tutorials, etc. It is especially popular for enterprise systems, that is, for systems that support the business process of complex organisations. It can be verbose.

JavaScript is a natural choice for web applications. There is a huge range of frameworks and libraries, so that the process of learning JavaScript is arguably more about learning some of its frameworks. JavaScript is dynamically typed, but if that is a problem for you you might want to consider TypeScript, which is essentially a statically typed variant of JavaScript, which compiles down to JavaScript. Be aware that the "Java" in "JavaScript" is there essentially for historical marketing reasons: when JavaScript came out, in 1995, Java was new and fashionable. The two languages are very different.

MATLAB is a language for numerical computing, widely used by scientists and engineers. Unlike most of the languages in this list, it has no open-source implementation.

Perl Perl stands for practical extraction and report language, or for pathologically eclectic rubbish lister. A Perl motto is "There's more than one way to do it." Once you know the language well, it is extremely convenient for many tasks, especially those that involve interacting with the operating system and manipulating strings. But it can be difficult to track down bugs in your Perl programs. I love Perl (which is really why it's in this list: it's not commonly taught as a first programming language, though you may come across it in passing, almost anywhere) but I find it hard to argue for you learning it now, unless you have existing Perl code to maintain. Do at least consider using Python instead.

PHP is a scripting language, widely used for web development (especially server-side scripting). It is easy to get started with, and is popular in web applications courses that have to cover a lot of ground. It has a reputation as a language which tends to encourage the writing of unmaintainable, insecure code – but this may be somewhat unfair, especially as recent versions of the language have improved.

Prolog is an old language which is having a resurgence with the AI boom. It has similar pattern-matching to functional languages like Haskell, but otherwise feels quite different from any of the other languages in this list: it's described as a logic programming language, and the fundamental idea is that you encode some facts and then ask questions about them.

Python By some measures Python is the most popular first programming language. I still rather resent Python for stealing the place in the language ecosystem that used to be occupied by Perl, one of my all-time favourite languages. There's no denying, though, that Python has many advantages over Perl. Perhaps the easiest way to summarise the difference is to point out that one of the principles included in the Zen of Python[2] is "There should be one – and preferably only one – obvious way to do it."[3]

Python is very easy to get started with, very popular, and a good all-purpose language. It's not statically typed, which means you may regret it if your program gets big and complicated. It's a popular language for data science and for machine learning, and has good facilities for manipulating strings. Its popularity means that there are libraries and frameworks for everything. There are significant differences between Python versions 2 and 3, so be sure you know which you are to use.

R is a language for doing statistics with data. It provides convenient facilities for graphing and analysis. Unlike MATLAB, which is sometimes used for the same tasks, it is an open-source language.

Racket/Scheme Widely used as a teaching language, but not so popular commercially, Scheme is a functional language from the Lisp family. Racket, originally a renaming of a version of Scheme, is now more popular. It has a minimalist language design philosophy, and is a good language to learn if you're interested in how programming languages work.

Since all of these languages are widely used, and most of them often act as first programming languages, there is good teaching material in all of them. Experiment!

14.3 The Changing Landscape of Languages

All of the languages in the previous section date back to the last century. But new programming languages are being invented all the

---

2 www.python.org/dev/peps/pep-0020/
3 Although that way may not be obvious at first unless you're Dutch.

time, and there are many other old ones I could have mentioned, too. You might like to search

 programming languages *this_year*

as well as, of course, watching out for information on which languages are used by people and organisations whose work you find interesting. The TIOBE index[4] attempts a regularly updated summary of the popularity of programming languages – but, unsurprisingly, its methodology is contested.

Above all, be aware that if you plan to have a career that involves programming, the language you learn first is unlikely to be the one you use most in your life. It is important to learn to write good programs in your first language, but it is equally important to set yourself on the path towards writing good programs in languages that have not yet been invented. To do this, make a habit of thinking about the why, as well as the what, of your programming decisions.

---

4 www.tiobe.com/tiobe-index/

15

How to Go Beyond This Book

This book has been aimed at students and their teachers engaged in early programming courses, and I hope you have found it useful. Once you've thoroughly absorbed its content, what next?

15.1 Doing More Programming

You can, of course, simply go ahead and write a program you find interesting. If you want a bit more structure to your practice, you might consider

- online coding challenges and contests, such as those found at HackerRank[1] – these are available in multiple languages, and you can do them competitively or just for fun;
- getting involved in outreach activities, e.g. helping with a coding club for school children: having to explain things is excellent for your own understanding;
- attending hackathons – intense, group programming events often organised by large employers or university societies – talks, etc., if you are lucky enough to be somewhere where these happen;
- contributing to an open-source project: projects that welcome newcomers often have a forum or a Get Involved page or similar to help you get started, and the website UpForGrabs[2] collates links to such projects.

The rest of this chapter is about books. If you have access to a university library, you are likely to find most of them there.

---

1 www.hackerrank.com
2 https://up-for-grabs.net/

15.2 Specific Programming Languages

You have probably been using an introductory book on your chosen programming language alongside this one. Most books treat their chosen language starting at the very basics, and include some material on how to write good programs in that specific language. There are so many of these books for each popular language that I'm not going to attempt to recommend specific ones. Indeed, because there are so many, you will usually find that you can indulge your own preferences for book style. Some people like short, terse books that explain each thing once. Others prefer discursive books that return to important topics and include lots of exercises. Browse, read reviews, ask for recommendations, and pick your favourite.

There are fewer books that focus on how to become an excellent programmer in some language. One such is Joshua Bloch's *Effective Java*. Once you have understood the basics of Java, this will be very useful.

15.3 Programming Generally

There's a plethora of books aimed at professional programmers, which may now be useful to you. Here are a few of my favourites.

Clean Code: A Handbook of Agile Software Craftsmanship by Robert C. Martin, known as "Uncle Bob". Active as a consultant, he also has a lot of material online; have a search.

Andrew Hunt and David Thomas's book *The Pragmatic Programmer* also includes lots of good stuff. Its subtitle "from journeyman to master" is a good indication of its target audience – you should already be a somewhat competent programmer to get much out of it – though it should be noted that it's not only men who can master programming! I believe it was the first edition of this book that introduced the term "kata", mentioned in Chapter 10, to programming.

Another popular book aimed at experienced programmers is Steve McConnell's *Code Complete*.

Rather different is the collection of chapters edited by Andy Oram and Greg Wilson, *Beautiful Code: Leading Programmers Explain How They Think*. The chapters take a variety of different approaches to the brief: you'll certainly find some of them thought-provoking.

Somewhat more algorithm-focused, though now dated, are Jon Bentley's classic *Programming Pearls* and *More Programming Pearls*. You might enjoy Gayle McDowell's *Cracking the Coding Interview* for its challenging small programming problems, even if you are not preparing for an interview.

15.4 Software Engineering

"Software engineering" is the term we use for all the processes and skills that contribute to ensuring that we have software available that meets our needs. The term seems probably to have been coined by Margaret Hamilton, who led a team developing software for the Apollo 11 space mission, in the early 1960s. It was popularised by its use in the titles of the NATO Conferences on Software Engineering in 1968 and 1969. The intention was to conjure up an idea of software being built in a systematic, reliable way, based on mathematics. The people building the software would be engineers, with the connotation that they would have undergone a certain kind of rigorous education, probably leading to a professional certificate. This was always more aspiration than reality – the very softness of software has always meant that people have built software without such an education. Nevertheless, we undoubtedly want well-engineered software, and an important step towards that is to understand how to write *good* programs, as discussed in this book and in those mentioned in the previous section.

Going beyond programming, software engineering also involves many other activities. There are whole fields that study how you manage the requirements of a system, including reconciling the conflicts between what different people want; how you can be sure you have done enough testing to be confident that your system is correct; and especially, how you can design the system so that it will be possible to maintain its usefulness while the world around it changes. Change is the root of the difficulty of software engineering. We mentioned in Chapter 10 that you should try to place things that will change at the same time close together in your program. This idea has been raised to an art form in the field of *design patterns*; the classic book is the so-called Gang of Four book (Gamma et al., 1994).

In order to think clearly about design, we need a way to represent the information that we need to focus on, while leaving out all the other information about the system which is irrelevant right now. For example, while thinking about the design structure of an object-oriented system, we might use a diagram that shows the classes in a system and the relationships between them, but leaves out all the detail of what the methods in the classes do. The same applies to many of the other important aspects of software development: in order to think about one aspect, we need a representation that shows the information we need, while leaving out what we do not need. Such a representation is called a model.

Terminology: Model

A *model* is an abstract, usually graphical, representation of some aspect of the system.

The use of models has been gradually increasing, and I think will become even more important in decades to come. My first book, *Using UML*, was about the Unified Modeling Language, which is now ubiquitous as a diagrammatic way to describe the design of systems. However, that language is complicated and can be frustrating. The future of modelling seems likely to involve using more, simpler modelling languages, which may be diagrammatic or textual, together with tools that process them automatically, rather as compilers do for programs. A plethora of books about this *model-driven engineering* have been appearing in the last few years. One of my favourites is *Model-Driven Software Engineering in Practice* by Marco Brambilla *et al.*

In a programming course, you are usually presented with clearly described requirements that won't change as you develop the program; if you work in a team with others at all, it will probably be a small team over a small length of time. In real-life software development, it is difficult to determine the requirements and they change over time. Large software systems often require very large teams of people with different skills. Managing all that is the subject of many books about software process. Two classics that it makes sense to read at a relatively early stage are Fred Brooks's *The Mythical Man-Month* – which made famous the observation that adding people to a software project that is late will often make it later – and Tom DeMarco and Timothy Lister's *Peopleware*, which, in a highly readable way, discusses the importance of the human characteristics of people involved in software development. Finally, you might also enjoy the book that started the agile revolution, Kent Beck's *Extreme Programming Explained: Embrace Change*.

15.5 Programming Language Theory

What none of the kinds of books we've discussed so far do much of, is comparing languages, and discussing their design and their properties. This is a fascinating topic, and understanding something about it can help you become a better programmer. Moreover, you may find yourself designing a language some day – *domain-specific languages* are becoming more common, so more programmers will find themselves involved in language design, at least of simple languages, than hitherto.

A great place to start is Shriram Krishnamurthi's book *Programming Languages: Application and Interpretation*. By carefully guiding you through writing an interpreter for a language, it helps you understand many of the choice points in language design.

As you learn more, advanced programming language theory books begin to become accessible to you. One of the best known is Benjamin Pierce's book *Types and Programming Languages*; if you're mathematically inclined, and want to know about type systems, this is well worth a read. Another of my favourites is Glynn Winskel's *Formal Semantics of Programming Languages*. Books in this category can be seriously challenging, though, so do browse in a library or bookshop to ensure you know what you are getting into, before you buy.

Bibliography

Brambilla, Marco, Jordi Cabot, and Manuel Wimmer. *Model-Driven Software Engineering in Practice*. Morgan and Claypool, 2017.

Beck, Kent. *Extreme Programming Explained: Embrace Change*. Addison-Wesley, 1999.

Bentley, Jon. *More Programming Pearls* , Facsimile edition. Addison-Wesley Professional, 1988.

Bentley, Jon. *Programming Pearls*, 2nd edn. Dorling Kindersley, 2006.

Bloch, Joshua. *Effective Java*. Addison-Wesley Professional, 2017.

Brooks, Frederick P. Jr. *The Mythical Man-Month: Essays on Software Engineering*, Anniversary edition. Addison Wesley, 1995.

Christiansen, Tom, Brian D. Foy, Larry Wall, and Jon Orwant. *Programming Perl*, 4th edn. O'Reilly Media, 2012.

Corbyn, Zoë. Interview: Margaret Hamilton: "They worried that the men might rebel. They didn't". *The Guardian*, July 2019. www.theguardian.com/technology/2019/jul/13/margaret-hamilton-computer-scientist-interview-software-apollo-missions-1969-moon-landing-nasa-women.

Dijkstra, Edsger W. *Notes on Structured Programming*, Technical report 70-WSK-03, 2nd edn, April 1970. www.cs.utexas.edu/users/EWD/ewd02xx/EWD249.PDF.

DeMarco, Tom and Timothy Lister. *Peopleware: Productive Projects and Teams*. Addison-Wesley, 2016.

Feynman, Richard P. Cargo cult science. *Engineering and Science*, 37(7), June 1974. http://calteches.library.caltech.edu/51/2/CargoCult.htm. Caltech's 1974 commencement address.

Fowler, Martin. *Refactoring: Improving the Design of Existing Code*. Addison-Wesley, 1999.

Gamma, Erich, Richard Helm, Ralph Johnson, and John Vlissides. *Design Patterns: Elements of Reusable Object-Oriented Software*. Addison-Wesley, 1994.

Heinlein, Robert A. *The Moon Is a Harsh Mistress*. G. P. Putnam's Sons, 1966.

Hoare, Tony. The emperor's old clothes. *Communications of the ACM*, 24(2):75–83, February 1981.

Hunt, Andrew and David Thomas. *The Pragmatic Programmer*. Addison-Wesley, 1999.

Knuth, Don. Notes on the van Emde Boas construction of priority deques: An instructive use of recursion, March 1977. Available via https://staff.fnwi.uva.nl/p.vanemdeboas/knuthnote.pdf.

Krishnamurthi, Shriram. *Programming Languages: Application and Interpretation*, 2nd edn. http://cs.brown.edu/courses/cs173/2012/book/, 2017.

Martin, Robert C. *Clean Code: A Handbook of Agile Software Craftsmanship*. Prentice Hall, 2008.

McConnell, Steve. *Code Complete*. Microsoft Press, 2004.

McDowell, Gayle Laakmann. *Cracking the Coding Interview*. CareerCup, 2015.

Oram, Andy and Greg Wilson, editors. *Beautiful Code: Leading Programmers Explain How They Think*. O'Reilly Media, 2007.

Pierce, Benjamin C. *Types and Programming Languages*. MIT Press, 2002.

Rainsberger, J. B. Putting an age-old battle to rest, December 2013. https://blog.thecodewhisperer.com/permalink/putting-an-age-old-battle-to-rest.

Raymond, Eric S. How to ask questions the smart way, 2014. www.catb.org/esr/faqs/smart-questions.html.

Stevens, Perdita and Rob Pooley. *Using UML: Software Engineering with Objects and Components*. Addison-Wesley, 2005.

van Rossum, Guido, Barry Warsaw, and Nick Coghlan. PEP 8 – style guide for Python code, July 2001. www.python.org/dev/peps/pep-0008/.

Winskel, Glynn. *Formal Semantics of Programming Languages*. MIT Press, 1993.

Index

A **bold** page number indicates where a term is defined.